RADIOHEAD
FROM A GREAT HEIGHT

STEVE DOUBLE / S.I.N.

RADIOHEAD
FROM A GREAT HEIGHT

JONATHAN HALE

ECW PRESS

The publication of *Radiohead* has been generously supported by the Government of Canada through the Book Publishing Industry Development Program.

CANADIAN CATALOGING IN PUBLICATION DATA

Hale, Jonathan, 1975–
Radiohead: from a great height
Includes bibliographical references.

ISBN 1-55022-373-9

1. Radiohead (Musical group) 2. Rock Groups – England. I. Title.

ML421.R129H162 1999 782.42166'092'2 C99-930324-4

The text of this book is set in Meta Plus Book with the display set in Letter Gothic

Desktop composition by Platinum Manuscript Services

Design by Guylaine Régimbald

Front cover photo: James A. Steinfeldt
Back cover photo: James A. Steinfeldt
Printed by Printcrafters, Inc., Winnipeg, Manitoba.

Distributed in Canada by General Distribution Services, 325 Humber College Boulevard, Etobicoke, Ontario M9W 7C3.

Distributed in the United States by LPC Group, 1436 West Randolph Street, Chicago, Illinois, U.S.A. 60607.

Distributed in the United Kingdom by Turnaround Publisher Services, Unit 3, Olympia Trading Estate, Coburg Road, Wood Green, London N2Z 6TZ.

Published by ECW PRESS
2120 Queen Street East, Suite 200
Toronto, Ontario M4E 1E2.
www.ecw.ca/press

PRINTED AND BOUND IN CANADA

acknowledgments

Radiohead, for me, is the greatest band ever formed, and writing this book was one of the best experiences of my life. First and foremost, I would like to thank Robert Lecker of ECW Press for giving me this opportunity. I'd also like to thank some other helpful people who work at the company: Holly Potter, Megan Ferrier, Jennifer Trainor, Guylaine Régimbald, and Paul Davies. A huge thanks goes out to two invaluable editors: Stuart Ross (chow down) and Mary Williams.

In researching this book, I met many very interesting and generous people who were more than happy to help me out. Jamie Lynn, Shaun Curtis, and John Mackelden all assisted in the preliminary stages. A very special thank-you to the three men who went to school with the members of Radiohead: Rick Clark (who answered an enormous number of questions); Alex Martyn (the school's photographer, who provided many incredible early pictures); and Simon Cranshaw (who generously offered to answer any questions I might have). Very special thanks go to sHack, who gave me great insight into Thom's college years. And to James Thomas, who I can't thank enough for putting me in contact with sHack (I still owe you one). I would also like to thank Clare Kleinedler for making time in her busy schedule to answer some questions for me. I am grateful to James Graham for allowing me to peruse many magazines from his vast collection; these were extremely helpful. Thanks, as well, to Drugstore's number-one fan, Adam V.H. Richards, whose Web site can be found at:

http://www.roblang.demon.co.uk/Drgstore/index.html

I interviewed members of Radiohead twice. The first time, I interviewed Jonny for the *University of Western Ontario Gazette*. The interview was conducted on 15 March 1996, by phone. Jonny was overseas at the EMI offices. The second interview was with Ed, Phil, and Colin for *Scene* magazine. This interview took place in a Toronto hotel room on 2 June 1997. Both of these interviews are cited throughout the book.

Thanks, also, to everyone who has been so supportive of me in this and other endeavors: Angela Whitehead (I couldn't ask for a better friend), Sandy, my mother and father, Bob Klanac, Matt Ireland, Todd Gaynor, Robert Thompson, Rob Gray, Tom Everett, Jason Ménard, Mike McCann, the UNB graduating class of 2001, and especially Kevin Kindred, Suzanne Bouclin, Coleen Harrington, Karin McLay, everybody at Loeb Southside, Mike D'Angelo, and all of my family and friends.

One thing that I have learned over the course of this project (and the years that I have been a fan of Radiohead) is that this band's followers bond (especially online) in a wonderful way that is truly unique. I would like to thank all of the friendly and generous tape traders and all of the intelligent, well-informed Web site owners I have encountered. A special thank-you is extended to Jonathan Percy for generously helping me out. His site can be found at http://radiohead.zoonation.com

Lastly, and most importantly, there are two people who deserve a special thank-you. Mark Pytlik not only wrote the opening portion of chapter 11, a description of his experiences at Glastonbury 1997, but also offered help or ideas or support whenever needed. And my sister, Jennifer. I really can't put into words how much I want to thank you. I thank you for introducing me to Radiohead in 1993, for being so supportive of everything I do, and for always helping me achieve my goals. It was your faith and help that allowed me to create this book.

Radiohead: From a Great Height is dedicated to all the Radiohead fans in the world, and to the band members themselves.

table of contents

INTRO-
DUCTION

Michael Eavis is a legend in the history of music festivals. In 1970, the Glastonbury farmer decided to hold a summer concert in a field he owned simply because he felt that England needed the sort of outdoor show he might be able to offer. It looked as though his idea would become a reality when the Kinks agreed to play — Ray Davies and the boys were bound to draw a fair-sized crowd. But the Kinks pulled out at the last minute. Eavis, instead of pulling the plug, enlisted Marc Bolan and T. Rex to take their place.

Over 2,000 people packed Eavis's field. Glastonbury Fayre was so successful that it inspired the farmer to hold another festival the following year. At that show, David Bowie, Traffic, and Hawkind took the stage, and over 10,000 people cheered them on. By the 1980s the festival's momentum was growing. Artists like New Order, the Smiths, the Waterboys, and Style Council all played major roles at Glastonbury throughout the decade, and the audience continued to expand. By the end of the decade, over 50,000 people jammed this summer-festival phenomenon.

Farmer Eavis's Glastonbury festival still has the power to pluck a band out of relative obscurity and transform it into a huge success. The best example occurred in 1995. Headliners the Stone Roses pulled out, allowing Pulp to fill this prestigious position. The band's acclaimed album *Different Class* had not yet been released, and at Glastonbury they found themselves playing to a crowd of over 80,000 on the strength of their previous album and the single "Common People." When the crowd sang along with that song and cried and cheered with every new, unreleased tune, Pulp went from being a popular band in England to becoming a huge international hit. The sales of their next album confirmed this new status.

Over time, Glastonbury has become one of the world's most im-portant festivals. The shows are covered by newspapers on every continent. Mainstream acts like the Spice Girls, Michael Jackson, or the Backstreet Boys are shunned, while envelope-pushing artists such as Sonic Youth, the Velvet Underground, and Blur are invited to headline. Glastonbury headliners are assigned the all-important task of closing a day filled with the sounds of several bands per-forming on three different stages, and the audience has never been let down.

In 1996, Radiohead's second album, *The Bends*, became a top-five hit, spurred on by the attention and critical acclaim the band had received at the end of the previous year and by the release of the exceptional single "Street Spirit (Fade Out)." This success had boost-ed the band's popularity in the world of British music, and, for the rest of the year, while Radiohead was tucked away in either Oxfordshire or Bath recording a third album, anticipation grew.

In 1997 Glastonbury organizers decided to gamble: they did not release the lineup for the festival to the public. Instead, they kept everyone guessing. They wanted to see whether people would still buy tickets for the show. Eavis's festival had been consistently selling out over the past several years, and, given the fact that the musical climate in Britain had been heating up, fans knew they could expect an exceptional show no matter who made the bill. But could the per-formers live up to such expectations?

Radiohead was secretly offered the festival's headlining Saturday-night slot. Although this was a wonderful achievement for the band, lead singer Thom Yorke couldn't enjoy it. He was worried. Radiohead had never played to such a large crowd as headliners. Suddenly it seemed as though the success that the band had achieved with *The Bends* came with unexpected challenges and pressures — the Glastonbury show would be used to promote an album that would only have been on store shelves for two weeks.

But in the eyes of fans and critics alike, Radiohead had, for the most part, only ever made music that pushed the boundaries of the mainstream. With its poignant lyrics and wealth of musical talent, the band could do no wrong, and when the rumor began to circulate that the Oxford five was set to headline at Glastonbury a wave of sheer excitement rippled through the music world.

After the release of Radiohead's third album, *OK Computer*, glow-ing reviews poured in from all over the world. This life-altering, impeccable masterpiece would, it was said, completely change the face of music. Band members smiled at such comments, but merely shrugged off most of what was said.

No amount of comforting and confidence building could elevate the mood of Thom Yorke. The promotion and the preview concerts for OK Computer filled his days as he fretted over the idea of playing in front of the Glastonbury crowd on 28 June. And, unfortunately, fate has a way of fulfilling the worrier's nightmares.

* * *

On the Wednesday before the festival, concertgoers start to show up at Eavis's site to stake a prime spot for their tents. They start partying in the summer sun. Just before six in the evening, the rain begins, and the weather only gets worse from this point on. It seems that this "summer sun festival" might not live up to its name, but the campers make the best of the situation. Radiohead, meanwhile, is off in another country promoting OK Computer.

The following day, thousands more people arrive at the site, ignoring the increasingly dismal weather conditions. After all, whatever the weather, there will still be a great lineup of bands. On the same day, Radiohead plays the Roskilde Festival in Denmark.

By Friday, many of the tents have lost their struggle against the storms, and the once-grassy Glastonbury site resembles a soaked, muddy battlefield. As the concert begins, the main-stage acts try to evoke a bit of excitement from the fans with various brands of intriguing music, but many in the audience are instead wondering if standing a foot deep in slippery mud is really the best way to spend their weekend. To make matters worse, the Other Stage, set up for performances by the Divine Comedy, Kenickie, and Ben Folds Five has been shut down. And weather conditions have prevented some bands from even making it to the festival. When the day's headliners, Prodigy, finally take the stage, they encounter technical difficulties so great that they are unable to give the kind of intense performance they are known for. Day one is over, and, for the most part, Glastonbury is making headlines all over the world — but these headlines have more to do with Mother Nature than with the music.

By Saturday, the weather hasn't let up at all. Radiohead members walk off their plane at Heathrow Airport and head straight to their tour manager's parents' house in Tilford, where they prepare themselves for their Glastonbury experience. Luckily, a country outfitter is situated next door, so they dash over to equip themselves with the outdoor gear they'll need to survive. From there, it's off to Glastonbury, where

Radiohead will play its first official show in England in 1997. Band members are not only nervous about the size of the crowd, but they also feel the pressure of delivering an album-launching performance on their home turf.

They are unaware of what has gone on throughout the weekend as they arrive at the weather-destroyed site. Only a few hours remain before the band takes the stage. All but Thom appear fairly at ease with the immediate situation — Colin talks to his friends in Massive Attack while the others mingle backstage.

As the night pushes forward, Radiohead finally takes the stage. They open with familiar tracks, starting with "Lucky" and moving right into "My Iron Lung," before attempting the new *OK Computer* songs. "Airbag" is a success, but things soon begin to fall apart. Throughout the first few songs of the set, Thom can see nothing but shining lights, which become even brighter by the fifth song. His monitors are shut off, so he can't hear what his bandmates are playing. Then the other monitors start to fail. Wrong notes are played. Tension builds among the band members. Thom considers leaving the stage and calling it quits, but the others talk him into staying. After almost every song, Thom yells at the sound man, but this proves futile. No band could imagine a worse experience.

British journalists, many of whom have a reputation for cruelty when it comes to reviewing bands, are very direct about Radiohead's performance. Gareth Grundy of *Select* magazine writes that "for 90 minutes, you forget about the conditions. The mud could've been neck deep and you wouldn't have given a monkey's because the soundtrack's so sublime. The new U2? Don't be so insulting . . ." ("Swamp Songs").

* * *

Radiohead's performance would stay in the minds of everyone who saw it — an intense concert experience. Radiohead was the band of the festival. History had been made. The muddy, devastated fields of Glastonbury had showcased a performance that might never be topped. And it had all been initiated 12 years earlier in the town of Oxford by five boys, brought together by their love for music, whose intellects, warm hearts, and quirky sensibilities would eventually touch many people's lives.

This is the story of Radiohead.

THE SOUND OF A BRAND-NEW WORLD

1

Jonny Greenwood, one of Radiohead's three guitarists, recently told a journalist, "The thing you have to remember is that we're English. We're not raised to talk about ourselves or to be overly emotional or sincere. Especially in public — or in private" (Gaitskill). He was describing what happens in most of the band's interviews. Radiohead members have not deliberately hidden information about their past, about the period of the band's formation, but — unlike the Eddie Vedders and Kurt Cobains of the American music scene, whose childhood experiences and family problems figure prominently in stories of their bands' development — these musicians are not overly explicit about their early years. One reason may simply be that no terrifying childhood experiences scarred them for life. This is not to say their childhoods haven't had an impact on their music or on Thom Yorke's lyrics — looking at what the lead singer/lyricist/guitarist went through in his youth, we get a sense of how much strength it took for him to overcome the cruelty of his playground peers. Becoming the musical genius he is today took a lot of hard work and devotion. But before we get too far into the influences that helped shape Radiohead we should go back to the beginning. The very beginning.

* * *

In the small town of Wellingborough, England, then home to approximately forty thousand people, Thom Edward Yorke was born on 7 October 1968. Thom would not live there for long — his childhood would be spent in Scotland where his father sold chemical-engineering equipment.

He passed much of his first five years in a hospital undergoing eye operations: he had been born with his left eye completely paralyzed, the lid permanently shut. By the age of six, Thom had undergone eye surgery five times. After his first operation, performed when he was still learning to speak, Thom looked at his parents and asked, "What have I got?" He recalls, "I woke up and I had this huge thing on my eye, and according to my parents, I just doubled up and started crying" (Malins, *Coming Up for Air*).

During yet another operation, he had a muscle grafted in to allow the eye to open. In the course of the final operation the doctors damaged the eye, leaving Thom half-blind. Perhaps attempting to cover up what might have been a mistake on their part, they told Thom's parents the eye had become "lazy" after so many operations. They gave Thom a patch to shield the fragile eye. To this day, he still has a sight problem. "I can kind of see," he notes. "I can judge if I am going to hit something, but that's just about it" (Malins, "Scuba Do").

The operations and the patch didn't help Thom to make friends at school, especially at an age when children tend to torment their vulnerable peers. Reflecting on the patch, Thom says, "It was a thing in the seventies that if you had unbalanced eyesight, [doctors] put a patch on to encourage the weak eye. If you wore one when you were six, you got teased a lot" (Sullivan). Sadly, the worst had yet to come.

In the short period Thom's family spent in Scotland, they lived near a beach that still contained mementos of the Second World War; bombers and barbed wire were embedded in the sand. In his spare time, Thom's father, who had been a boxing champion at university, tried to teach his son the sport. Thom recalls being knocked over quite often by his father during these "training" sessions. Though he never became a skilled boxer, Thom learned enough to ensure that he never had to back down from a fight at school.

In Scotland, Thom was also first introduced to music. At the age of four, he received an acoustic guitar. Unfortunately, it was a steel-string guitar, and he cut his fingers open playing it. Frustrated, he smashed the instrument against a wall, destroying it. But music wasn't really young Thom's greatest interest. Instead, he spent a fair bit of time building Lego models and displaying them to his family. He was always eager to hear people's opinions of these creations — even at this early stage Thom's creative side, his need to express himself, was beginning to shine forth. He desired an audience.

At seven, while wearing the eye patch, Thom met a girl who proved intelligent and loving enough to look beyond the physical features that so many others just couldn't ignore. Katie Ganson became Thom's first girlfriend; he sensed she would also be his one and only.

With her, Thom experienced his first French kiss, but, as fate would have it, before the year was over his parents decided it was time for the family to move. Thom and Katie professed their love for one another and agreed to get married one day, but they were never to see each other again. Along with his younger brother, Andy, Thom was hauled off to Oxford.

Katie was one of the last people to cherish Thom's truly formidable qualities for a long time. At the Standlake Church of England School in Oxford, Thom would have to endure his lowest point yet — the new boy with the eye patch quickly became a target for mockery.

At the age of eight, though, Thom's life changed for the better. He and a friend went to a record store and his friend purchased *Queen's Greatest Hits*. This was Thom's first musical memory (aside from the painful steel-string guitar experience). After listening to the album, he set himself a new goal in life: he would learn to play just like Brian May. "Bohemian Rhapsody" blew Thom's mind, since the only music in his house was an album of Scottish dance tunes. His mother gave him a Spanish guitar, and Thom began taking lessons, intent on fulfilling his dream. But his guitar teacher laughed at his aspirations, and despite his effort and dedication Thom could only manage to play "Kumbaya."

Over the next two years, Thom found himself drawn into many more fights, but he mostly kept to himself, retreating to the school's music room. Without learning how to read music, he improved his guitar playing so much that at the age of ten he formed his first band. It was a short-lived enterprise for two reasons, one being the very unique but dangerous undertaking of his partner: he took apart old television sets, presumably to create percussion instruments. This led to several electric shocks and put a sudden end to the duo's career. The second reason the band was short-lived was that Thom's parents enrolled him in Abingdon Boys' School in Abingdon, Oxfordshire. Here, because of his eye, he was given the nickname Salamander. Notes Thom: "It was a very malicious school and everyone had very malicious nicknames, so Salamander was par for the course" (Sutherland, "Material World").

Though the boxing lessons Thom had received from his father should have come in handy at this time, his training hadn't included advice on how to win. Thom found himself on the hurting end of many fights during his Abingdon days. "I was a fighter at school," he says, "but I never won. I was into the idea of fighting" (Doyle, "Party On"). It wouldn't be until Thom reached Exeter University that he would develop an aversion to fighting.

15

Thom came to realize that his problems were not limited to his vic-timization by other children. A new problem took the form of an Abingdon figure he would grow to despise: the school's headmaster, Michael St. John Parker. Parker, too, was awarded a nickname by the children. He was "the Beak," because he had a "nose that would have given Pinocchio a run for his money on a lie-filled day," former Abingdon student Rick Clark explained to me.

Thom describes Parker as "a power crazed lunatic who banned music and walked around in robes impersonating a bishop" (Morris). Clark elaborates, saying that Parker "constantly prowled the school grounds in his Dracula robes, trying to look like a slice of early-nine-teenth-century English school folklore."

Twice a week the students were sent to the school chapel to serve as an audience for Parker. Thom claims the man was never ordained as a minister, and by pretending to be one left an indelible impression on many of the students. His actions had such an impact on Thom that he later wrote a song about Parker, "Bishop's Robes." The head-master tormented Thom right up until his graduation in 1987.

Another memorable point in Thom's early education involved a cer-tain essay question he was assigned: "If you were an alien landing on Earth, how would you describe what you saw?" Thom found this question not just mind-blowing but also kind of funny; he could well imagine the huge laugh an alien would have when faced with the strange phenomenon of life on Earth. While we may never know what Thom actually wrote in response to that question, it would prompt him to pen a song many years later called "Subterranean Homesick Alien."

Despite his problems with school-yard bullies, Thom's heart was becoming enthralled by music, and at the age of eleven — only one year after his first band had split up — he wrote his first song, "Mushroom Cloud," which was about the way atomic explosions looked, not the horrible effects they had.

At twelve, Thom joined a punk outfit at school called TNT. This band would expand Thom's musical abilities, because when the time came to sing, all the other members shied away from the job, leaving him to fill the void. "I started singing into this little stereo mike tied to the end of a broomstick handle. Everyone just started falling about laughing, and that was that," explains Thom. "That was my introduc-tion to singing" (Morris).

Over the next year or so, TNT tried to hang together and create songs, but the various personalities involved began to clash, which ruined the experience for Thom. As the other members walked around with their large egos and attitudes, Thom walked away. Still wanting to be in a band, Thom decided to form his own group. He would find people who were about his own age and who also seemed to share in his passion for music, people who followed the less popular acts of the era, like Joy Division. There was one member of TNT with whom Thom felt a connection, however — one boy who wouldn't buy into the snobbery of the others. His name was Colin Greenwood, and Thom asked him to join his new musical project as bassist.

Colin Charles Greenwood was born in Oxford on 26 June 1969. When he was only two years old, an event took place that would alter both his life and that of Thom Yorke. His mother gave birth to his brother, Jonathan, on 5 November 1971. The two grew up as most siblings do, the older guiding the younger along, teaching him right from wrong. Em . . . well, maybe this was not always the case.

Jonathan was born color-blind, a condition Colin seems to have taken advantage of during these early years. When they painted pictures together, Colin would often switch around the colors in the paint box Jonny was using, causing him to create what have been described as "disturbing pictures." Colin discusses one such painting: "I gave [Jonny] a red crayon to use for the grass he was coloring. It was a blood bath" (Hendrickson). Recalling these experiences, Jonny jokes that Colin "retarded [him]" (Doyle, "Party On").

Jonny was exposed to music at a very young age by a number of family members, including his grandfather. "Me and my grandfather would play tunes together," he explains. "He'd sit me on his knee when I was three, and teach me how to play the banjo. And I remember saying one day, 'Enough of *My Fair Lady*!' And that's how rock 'n' roll was born" (Paphides).

The Greenwood house was a very musical environment (even though the boys' mother was tone-deaf), regularly filled with the sounds of *My Fair Lady*, the *Mikado*, *Grease*, and Mozart's Horn Concertos, to name but a few. And while this music was intriguing in its own way, it would be Jonny and Colin's eldest sister, Susan, who would have the greatest musical impact on the two brothers.

Susan introduced them to the cooler bands that she was into, many of them bands that most young people at the time were not really interested in. She also became a role model for the boys after their father passed away, when Colin was seven and Jonny was five. Colin credits Susan with keeping them in touch with the more vital artists, saying, "She's responsible for our precocious love of miserable music. The Fall, Magazine, Joy Division [and so on]. We were ostracized in school because everyone else was into Iron Maiden" (Hendrickson).

At six, Jonny started his record collection by purchasing Squeeze's "Cool for Cats" single, which had been pressed on pink vinyl. He soon learned the words, and often sang it for his mother and her friends. Around the same time, Jonny got a recorder, his first instrument. He loved to play it, and the instrument inspired him to play others in the years that followed. Soon, Jonny would dive into jazz guitar, the viola, and the piano. What is especially interesting about his desire to play all of these instruments is that he did not come from a musical family. Although the Greenwoods enjoyed music, there wasn't a musician among them, though Jonny has pointed out that his grandfather briefly played the euphonium, a brass wind instrument.

Colin didn't purchase his first guitar until he was in his early teens, but he proudly notes that he did so with his own money. His mother, despite the fact that she disapproved of her sons considering music as a career choice, always made sure she had a little extra money set aside for repairing guitar strings. At school, Colin wasn't as inclined as Thom to hide out in the music room, but the two still saw quite a lot of each other because they were in the same year and attended the same classes. They also ran into each other at many parties in the early 1980s, and it was at these gatherings that Thom first became drawn to Colin. Their conversations revealed that Colin had impeccable taste in music. His enthusiasm for the inspirational and passionate Joy Division bought the bassist a ticket to join Thom's group, on the condition that he try to fulfil one request. Thom wanted Colin to play the bass like Joy Division/New Order player Peter Hook. Thom claims this hasn't happened.

Yet Colin Greenwood was not the first person to join Thom's post-TNT project. The person who holds that distinction entered the scene in a more theatrical way. While at Abingdon, Thom got involved in the drama department. He was able to participate in several productions without having to act, because some plays required musical accompaniment — such as *A Midsummer Night's Dream*, staged in 1985. On one occasion, Thom and another student were up on a scaffolding positioned to play background music. When the two began jamming free-form jazz, their unimpressed instructor asked them what they were doing. As student actor Ed O'Brien, a witness to the incident, reports, Thom's reply was, "I don't know what the fuck we're supposed to be playing" (Doyle, "Party On"). This would be Ed's first musical experience with Thom, but obviously not his last: Ed was to be the first musician Thom recruited for his new project.

Edward John O'Brien was born in Oxford on 15 April 1968. His father, a doctor, sent him off to Abingdon. Here, at this boys-only private school, Ed learned cricket and improved his acting abilities, both of which played an important role in his adolescence. When he was ten, his parents split up. Ed lived with his mother, but maintained a close relationship with his father.

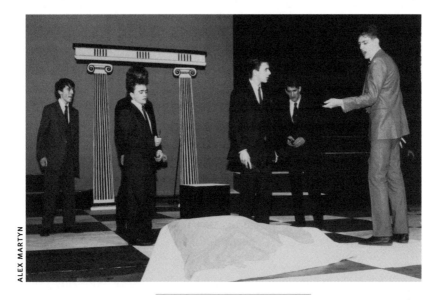

Ed O'Brien plays Brutus in a modern-dress version of *Julius Caesar*
Abingdon School, 1986

His interest in music was ignited in the summer of 1977, the year Elvis Presley died. Throughout that summer of Elvis tributes, Ed watched an endless procession of old Elvis movies on television. He suddenly knew he wanted to be a musician. At Abingdon, though, his fascination with the theater grew as strong as his interest in music.

Ed was quite an athlete, and remained a member of the school's cricket team for some time. But it was not on the playing field that the connection between Thom and Ed formed. Thom was drawn to Ed due to his resemblance to Morrissey, the Smiths' lead singer. Not only did Ed look like this soon-to-be British legend, but he also had an obsession with Morrissey and the Smiths that would continue through his teen years. It was this band's guitarist, Johnny Marr, who inspired Ed to pick up a six string early in the eighties.

Throughout this period, Thom continued to write new songs and perform for friends. While the instrumental aspect of the music was most important to Thom, he did jot down a few lyrics, and these prompted some criticism. Upon reading what Thom had written, one friend noted that Thom's lyrics were far too serious and personal. "[She] said, 'Your lyrics are crap. They're too honest, too personal, too direct, and there's nothing left to the imagination,'" says Thom. He adds, "I've had that in the back of my mind ever since" (Mueller).

The members of Thom's combo played their first gig at a friend's birthday party, but as they were only a three-piece group comprised entirely of guitar players, percussion had to be provided by a drum machine. Unfortunately, the machine — called "Dr. Rhythm" — broke down after the first song. Ed still recalls the obscenities that flew from Thom at the microphone as they scrambled to repair the machine. But all was lost. The gig impressed no one.

After the Dr. Rhythm fiasco, the threesome immediately set out to find a more reliable replacement. The drummer they set their sights on, a fellow Abingdon student, was already in a band of his own, Jungle Telegraph, but Thom, Colin, and Ed decided to make a grab for him anyway. Ed headed off to the pub the night after their ill-fated debut to ask Phil Selway, a year ahead of the trio at school, to join the band.

Phillip James Selway was born on 23 May 1967 in Hemmingford Grey, a small Cambridgeshire town. His introduction to music occurred early in life, and it startled his parents. "I found my first drum at 3 o'clock in the morning of my third Christmas," he explains. "My parents never really encouraged me to play after that" (Harkins).

Phil's interest in playing drums grew over time, though the only instrument he trained in was the tuba. His family moved to Oxford when he was still young, and he joined a few bands during his years at Abingdon School, leading up to Jungle Telegraph. Phil and his friends picked on the younger students, and some of them got to know Thom and Colin by beating them up. But Phil got along with Thom, Colin, and Ed, so Ed wasn't too intimidated to approach Phil that evening in the pub. He begged the older boy to join the new band.

Phil agreed to practice with the trio and see how it went. Thom's first words to Phil are imprinted on the memories of both musicians. Thom turned to Phil and asked, "Can't you play any fucking faster?" (Morris). Maybe it was the intensity of their performance or the love that these younger boys displayed for the music, but Phil overlooked his awkward introduction to Thom and decided to stay on.

The band practiced on Fridays, and so they came up with the name On a Friday. As the idea behind this musical venture was simply to have fun and play songs together, band members would sometimes ask other musicians to help out. While the core group was Thom, Ed, Phil, and Colin, their sound was filled out by a keyboardist.

Jonny also showed up at these practices, but because he was still so young he was mainly there so that his brother could keep an eye on him. After awhile he got tired of just sitting around and watching. "I was kind of the annoying younger brother hanging around and offering to play any instrument and learn anything to play with them," Jonny told me. "[I was] thirteen and [my brother] was sixteen and all of [his] friends are sixteen or seventeen and they are all tall and terrifying."

Still, Jonny was adamant that the band give him a chance, not only because he was bored just watching them, but also because he truly believed in what the older boys were doing and wanted to be a part of their future. "I'd heard tapes of Thom's songs before I joined," explains Jonny, "and I couldn't get over the fact that if I played an Elvis Costello record and then his stuff, the songs were as good. And yet he was sixteen and at my school" (Bailie, "Viva la Megabytes").

The practices were not as much about jamming together and working on new songs as they were about learning to play the instruments. Jonny sat and watched the older boys, always offering to fill in on an instrument if needed. His musical talent had greatly improved over the years; he had become a member of the Thames Valley Orchestra. But the group wasn't ready to let him in just yet.

Thom was writing more songs now, and he made some demos on his own. He also hauled his guitar around to parties. Not only was he passionate about playing, but he also loved the attention. All that time he'd spent in the music room had turned him into a talented guitarist. One former Abingdon student, Simon Cranshaw, remembers approaching Thom after buying a guitar to ask if the older boy would teach him how to play it. Thom sat down with him and showed him "Rebel Rebel" by David Bowie, telling him that if he could learn to play the song himself the lessons would continue.

Meanwhile, in his final years at Abingdon, Colin was living the rock-and-roll lifestyle, putting on makeup and sneaking off to see some of his favorite acts, including the Fall. He immersed himself in the crazy lifestyle of the music fan, and it was not unusual for him to sleep outdoors somewhere between his home and a gig.

While the band was a major part of the boys' lives, it was not the only thing that took up their spare time. As they grew older, they had to get jobs. In 1986, Ed worked in an Oxford pizza parlor, and there he encountered a very interesting customer. "I once served Stephen Hawking," he told me. "He came in and, I mean, I didn't know who he was at the time. I was on the bar, and the waitress was taking the order at the table next to the bar. And it was really amazing. I didn't know whether to laugh, 'cause obviously you didn't. . . ." Mimicking a computerized voice, Ed added, "It was like, 'ex-tra tu-na and ol-ives.'"

Phil, who had graduated from Abingdon in 1986, spent the next year working as a desk editor at an academic press. He didn't see the job as a career move, however: "Even though I've done other things, it's always been the band at the forefront" (Masuo).

The same year, two albums were released that would become important to the future of On a Friday. The first was Elvis Costello's *King of America*, which came out in February 1986. Later Thom realized that every track on the album was "about some extreme human emotion" ("Single to Damascus Please"). In "I'll Wear It Proudly," Costello sings of bitter feelings and a sense of loneliness, but declares in the chorus that he will proudly wear the crown to become the king of fools. The song is honest and direct, revealing an array of personal wounds. Its lyrics, like those of Thom's songs, allow the listener to identify strongly with the singer. Says Thom, "['I'll Wear It Proudly'] affected the way I wrote, because it was the first time I'd really heard anyone write about the things that I wanted to write about. The way he plays the track is just pure genius; just him and the acoustic guitar with these words and the organ is coming in and out and plays the song out. It's really upsetting, but I feel better afterwards, which is my ideal ingredient for a song" ("Single to Damascus Please").

The other 1986 album that had a profound effect on the band was Talking Heads' *True Stories*. "Radio Head," a catchy pop number, was released as a single. The role this song played later in the band's career is obvious.

All this time, Jonny was bugging band members to give him a shot. Finally, after being pestered for a full year, Colin told his younger brother to bring his harmonica to a practice. A week later, the band appeared at the Jericho Tavern in Oxford with Jonny on board.

Sitting at the edge of the stage, Jonny waited anxiously through a portion of the set, listening and watching the band bang out its first live gig for an audience not made up of schoolmates. Finally, Thom turned and gave him the nod, and Jonny lit into his harmonica. From that moment on, Jonny was an official member of On a Friday.

The band soon decided to expand even more, aiming for a fuller sound by recruiting two saxophonists from the Abingdon girls' school (and a male friend sometimes played a third sax). A keyboardist they had been using (whose playing was far too loud) was let go, and Jonny became his replacement. To ensure he would not meet the same fate as his predecessor, Jonny set the volume of the keyboard at zero and just hit the keys. The other band members didn't notice, and agreed that Jonny was adding wonderful effects to the songs.

As the practices continued, On a Friday honed a sound of its own, but, unfortunately, some songs were beginning to sound a little too much like REM, a band they all admired. Jonny described to me the band's reaction to this situation: "I remember this argument going on in the rehearsal room when we were practicing at school, and Ed was saying, 'Oh we sound just like REM,' and Thom said, 'Well, do you ever think they are going to get really big? Do you think anyone would notice that we sound like REM?' Colin was saying, 'No, they're not going to get any bigger,' but someone was saying, 'No, they're going to have their day.'" Whoever that final speaker was, it's a good thing that everyone listened, because REM's achievement of international acclaim and enormous sales was only a few years away.

In the final year of school for Ed, Colin, and Thom, more serious issues arose. The boys' parents didn't mind that they played in a band in their spare time, but a career in music just didn't figure in their plans for their children. And so the three, along with Phil, started applying to universities and colleges. Thom, whose studies had taken a back seat from the age of thirteen to fifteen, now began preparing for college. He took his studies during his final year at Abingdon very seriously. The subjects he excelled at — and would continue to pursue at university — were art and music.

"I got an art prize and a music prize, which is really funny 'cos I couldn't read music and I couldn't really paint," he says. "It was great, though — it was the first time I'd ever had any encouragement" (Sutherland, "Material World"). Thom was awarded a twenty-pound book token.

As the academic year drew to a close, the school staged its annual Symposium Revue, which was, Rick Clark explained to me, "a chance for the final-year students to put on a play to pillory the masters and the school." Ed was a part of the show, which included short plays or musical performances. So was Thom. Clark says that when Thom came out to play one of his own acoustic numbers, he "really impressed the audience."

So, their schoolboy days finally behind them, Ed, Phil, and Colin, looked ahead to college. Thom, however, had chosen to take a year off before furthering his education and his musical career.

YOU'D KILL YOURSELF FOR RECOGNITION

2

On 19 August 1987, 27-year-old Michael Robert Ryan, armed to the teeth, blazed through his hometown of Hungerford, Berkshire, on a murder spree. He killed one person in nearby Savernake Forest and several more in the town. Ryan shot seven people who lived on his street dead before heading into the center of town, where he killed many more. Cornered by police at the local school, Ryan took his own life. He'd killed 16 people before ending his inexplicable journey of destruction.

In the wake of this tragic event, Hungerford, population 4,800, shut down for the day. Then the shock of the massacre set in.

No one ever discovered what triggered Ryan's rampage, which had stunned much of England. Thom Yorke was seriously affected by the atrocity, and very soon afterwards he wrote a song to capture the feelings it had generated. Entitled "Sulk," it ended with the line "Just shoot your gun."

Overall, though, things should have been looking up for Thom at this time, simply because he was out of Abingdon and free of his nemesis, Headmaster Parker. But Thom had entered the sphere of a man as irritating and cruel as Parker — his boss at the shop where he sold suits.

Thom reminisces: "This guy was the floor manager of our department which was menswear. I couldn't afford any of the suits I was meant to be selling so I used to turn up in an Oxfam suit — which was quite smart — but I still had long blond hair and he took an instant dislike to me. He used to say, 'Why aren't you selling any suits?' and I'd say 'Because they're crap and nobody wants to buy them,' which didn't go down well. He's one of those blokes who'd drive to work, kill a cyclist and not stop" (Malins, *Coming up for Air*). When Thom was wrongfully accused of stealing a suit, he quit.

His personal life was also going through a rough patch — he and his current girlfriend fought a lot. He has admitted that because he attended a boys' school he feels awkward around women. Sadly, he now found himself in a dysfunctional relationship. While dating this girl, Thom's obsession with cars deepened. His parents had moved a fair distance out of Oxford, but as he was now old enough to drive, Thom could take his car into town to see his girlfriend. One day, while the two were in the car, they got into a terrible accident. Thom's girlfriend suffered whiplash, and Thom came face to face with the car's lethal potential. He became uncomfortable on the road, and it didn't help that his next car, a Morris Minor, had a door that wouldn't shut properly. Out on the highway, maintaining the speed limit due to the faulty door, Thom watched other cars racing by at reckless speeds. Luckily, he still had his music (Kleinedler, "Don't Call").

Jonny was still toiling at Abingdon. Colin was attending Peterhouse College, the oldest college at Cambridge University. That Colin had been admitted surprised everyone, including Colin himself. He hadn't even had the confidence, initially, to apply there. At Peterhouse Colin studied English, leading his mother to believe that her eldest son would go into law or accounting, or even become an academic. Phil entered Liverpool Polytechnic, where he studied English and history. Ed went off to Manchester University, not simply to take up residence in the hometown of the recently disbanded Smiths, but to study economics.

While their bandmates were away at school, Thom and Jonny wrote songs, taping them on a four-track in Jonny's bedroom. Thom admits that composing songs with Jonny made him more comfortable with writing lyrics — an activity he hadn't felt like bothering with for a long time.

In 1988, Thom finally entered Exeter University, where he studied English and art. Here he found himself surrounded by like-minded people, part of an environment that until then he hadn't believed could possibly exist. He could now unlearn everything that had been inflicted on him thus far in his schooling. He describes Exeter as a "finishing school for upper class idiots and one of the most exciting environments I'd ever been in" (*Interview Sessions*). Feeling lucky to be at the college and very content to be around people with whom he shared so much, Thom was convinced he had found a way to mold his creative side. In his first year, he took a job at the Lemon Grove, a campus bar; he was a DJ for the university's Big Club night, always held on Fridays. This gig gave him a good excuse to buy a ton of records, and it made him a cult figure on campus.

After his first week, over 200 people showed up to hear what Thom would spin at the Lemon Grove. As he was still equipped with only a handful of albums, he went out and bought many more — 250 pounds' worth — to vary his set for the swelling audience. Soon, over a thousand people were cramming the club on Friday nights.

One night, Thom recalls, "This madwoman came in and said, 'You have beautiful eyes, but they're completely wrong.' When I get paranoid, I just think of what she said" (Wiederhorn, "Radiohead").

Working as a security guard at the same bar was another Exeter student, a year ahead of Thom, who was doing a degree in music with a major in composition. Now known as sHack, this young musician would go on to form an outfit known as Lunatic Calm. He talked to me in 1998, offering much insight into Thom's time at Exeter. Recalling the success Thom had met with as a DJ, sHack explained that the year before Thom came to Exeter, Frank Tope (current editor of *Muzik* magazine) had been a DJ there, and while Tope had done a great job, he was "dedicated to his Rare Groove and his old Salsoul records, which wasn't really where the kids were at. Thom turned it around with a great mixture of indie tunes of the day mixed up with an educative influx of early hardcore gear. I remember getting there early for work so he could spin me what he'd bought that week — Ragga Twins, Shut Up and Dance, R and S stuff, Kickin' records. . . . He was really excited about what was happening in dance music. At the end of that year, the club was packed each Friday."

Thom and sHack became friends when they discovered that they shared many of the same political views and had similar musical tastes. As sHack notes, "Thom and I were very much into politics and the arts, and having established where you stood, you'd have a ready-made network of 300 to 400 like-minded people." They decided to form a band together, and called it Headless Chickens. When they found out that a New Zealand act had the same name, they simply became Headless.

"The whole thing was very much a college band — having a laugh but with an eye on taking it further," says sHack. "The lineup was me and Thom on vocals sharing lead and some harmony, with him playing guitar and me grappling with a bass and some keyboards. We then had John Matthias on electric violin as well as a drummer [who had] a penchant for wearing ladies' dresses and motorcycle helmets. On occasion, we'd draft in a second guitarist, Howie, [later a member of] Flicker Noise and now [part of] Lunatic Calm, and a second violinist, Laura Forest-Hay, who chipped in with the odd vocal." Continues

27

The young Phil Selway, London School of Economics, summer 1988

sHack: "We did dozens of live shows, and Thom and I were responsible for writing material jointly, which was one of the greatest buzzes I've had writing music. We just had this symbiosis when it came to generating ideas — tunes would take little more than an hour or so to put together. There was an anarchist collective that we helped form around the time in Exeter, called Hometown Atrocities, with the aim of raising money for rebel groups by putting on shows around town, and as it developed Headless became key players at those shows, supporting the likes of Snuff and Senseless Things."

Thom also became a member of the anti-fascist club at Exeter, and this, unfortunately, caused him to take up physical fighting again. Demonstrating outside of Exeter's football stadium one day, club members were surreptitiously photographed by the football team's supporters so that those involved could be identified and "punished." After some skinheads arrived on the scene bent on using violence as a means of ending the protest, Thom and his friends went home. "It wasn't a pleasant experience," says Thom (Hendrickson).

Aside from DJ-ing and playing in Headless, Thom was busy becoming a striking figure on campus by sporting an outsize coat and a "grandad hat." He admits to being into the New Romantic style when it was no longer fashionable. This look also got Thom into trouble. He drew the attention of two guys who saw him entering a bar one night. Noticing their stares, Thom blew the pair a kiss. This didn't go over too well: they beat the crap out of Thom. After this, his attraction to fighting dwindled.

As far as education was concerned, Thom found himself uninterested in his academic program during that first year, despite feeling solidarity with the people around him. He couldn't paint, and wasn't interested in the style of art being taught. When it came to his English courses, he saw no point in regurgitating what was already written in the books he was assigned. Since his professors had virtually told him he could do whatever he wanted, Thom decided he would do nothing.

Although he got little out of his first year, in his second year he was introduced to computers, Exeter's newly acquired Macs. He learned to scan images and overlay them to form new ones. Told that this wasn't art, Thom was not deterred, and continued to create pieces using this technique throughout his university career.

Later, Thom would reflect on this artistic undertaking, saying, "When I was in college the only artwork I ever really loved was something with this dodgy broad term of 'Outsider Art,' which was basical-

Thom at the London School of Economics
(in one of the band's first shows), summer 1988

ly by completely untrained people who'd never been to art college or who were mentally unstable. One of my favourite artists was this, uh, paedophilic bloke and he did these scribbles which most people would say were like the doodles you do [when you're on the] telephone." But, he continued, "There was something about the way he could pick up a pen and put it on a piece of paper, which sounds really wanky but I'd much rather study stuff like that than all the endless fucking Saatchi & Saatchi art, y'know — here's the New Artists For The 90s and aren't they wonderful? I'd much rather go off and explore stuff that didn't come out of that context at all, because that context is self-referential and boring" (Malins, *Coming Up for Air*).

The influence of that "paedophilic bloke" extended to Thom's music. One of the first songs in On a Friday's roster was "Nothing Touches Me," which, explains Thom, "is based on an artist who was imprisoned for abusing children and spent the rest of his life in a cell, painting, but the song is about isolating yourself so much that one day you realize you haven't got any friends anymore and no one talks to you" (Ronan).

Despite their hectic schedules, the four university men still returned to Oxford about once a month for a weekend of practicing, working on new material, and thinking up new band names — they had realized On a Friday was a terrible moniker. Ed says, "We were all at different universities around the country, and the commitment was pretty unbelievable in that we'd get back every three weekends. We'd all come back to Oxford, and Oxford's not — you know, I was in Manchester and Manchester's such a great city. Why would you want to leave Manchester for weekends when there's so much going on? The only reason was 'cause of the band" (Masuo).

Meanwhile, Thom's other musical interest, Headless, was taking on the dimensions of a serious project. The duo put out a limited-edition single titled "I Don't Wanna Go to Woodstock," which contained songs from a four-track sampler that sHack and Thom had done. The act almost released a proper single titled "Beautiful" — which, sHack says, "on reflection would have been very Radiohead had I not been intent on techno-ing it up" — but the tapes for the single were lost, and it was never released.

Reminiscing about this period when he and Thom regularly got together to listen to music and write it, sHack explains, "We were quite similar in that music was like a quest for the ultimate — be it structure, sonics, or melody. Nothing was more thrilling than getting it right, but at the same time it was largely about using music as a means of release. It was never a drag; it was always a case of expecting the unexpected, and I think we both used to look forward to bagging a few hours here and there where we could learn from each other — be it playing records we'd just bought, or writing songs."

Thom's other great interest at university was drinking. In fact, all members of On a Friday took to drinking heavily while at university. They also became involved with drugs. And though he says that his binges almost took his life, sHack remarks that Thom's drinking habits were actually par for the course. "As a student at Exeter, as I'm sure is the case anywhere, we all did our fair share of drinking. I remember one summer getting fucked up and crashing out in various beer gardens for seven full weeks without a day off. Thom was a part of that culture, although because he studied at the art college — which was on the other side of town — he was present less often than others around the main campus. I certainly don't remember him being any more or less of a caner than anyone else."

During one of his drinking binges, Thom wrote a song that would completely change his life. The song was "Creep." But, he insists, "I wasn't very happy with the lyrics; I thought they were pretty crap" (Kenny). "Creep" was about being in an alcoholic stupor and not having the confidence to talk to the people he really wanted to get to know.

Thom brought his drinking under tighter control when he became captivated by another Exeter student named Rachel. But given his limited experience with the opposite sex, he didn't pursue her in any normal way. "She really thought I was a freak," he admits. "She thought I was impossible to talk to, really moody, difficult, unpleasant and idiotic. And I think I was. But she bashed a lot of that crap out of me" (Stud Brothers). Thom respects Rachel's privacy by not talking about her, aside from relating the story of how they first got together. Was this relationship any more successful than Thom's previous one? The answer is yes: Thom and Rachel are still very happily together.

Meanwhile, at Cambridge, Colin was also partaking of the wild life, drinking and dating, but, like the others, he remained very serious about On a Friday. The elder Greenwood became his school's entertainment officer, a position he used to the band's advantage by getting them a couple of gigs at Cambridge. He was also able to pay the band quite handsomely. Colin notes that for these gigs they did a "nifty version of Elvis Costello's 'Pump It Up.'" "At one gig," Colin confides, "we had couples shagging on the lawn which I like to think was down to the seductive qualities of our music, but I'd say it had more to do with the amount of beer that'd been consumed" (Stuart Clark).

London School of Economics, summer 1988

Yet all of this extracurricular activity didn't keep Colin from his studies. He wrote a thesis on Raymond Carver, the American poet and short-story writer on whose work the 1992 Robert Altman film *Short Cuts* was based. His passion for reading and learning has never waned, and those who know him comment on his intelligence. But, unlike his Cambridge classmates, Colin never really felt the pressure to succeed at school, as he was convinced that, with a lot of hard work and devotion, his career path would lead to the music industry. After all, he had three very talented friends and a musical brother, and together they formed an original and intriguing band.

At home in Oxford, the younger Greenwood was still trying to finish up at Abingdon. He was also learning how to play guitar and had begun writing songs. Jonny started playing with Thom's younger brother, Andy, and the two formed a band at school. The project never really took off, but the experience was invaluable to Jonny. It would help him to write songs later on with Thom, and his improved guitar skills would greatly enhance On a Friday's sound. The experience was great for Andy, as well; he would go on to become guitarist and singer in the passionate trio the Unbelievable Truth.

Phil's extracurricular activity at school was to assist others as a Nightline operator. This service was set up to provide students with information on everything from calling a cab to dealing with sexual issues. As a referral service, Nightline directed callers to a number of help sources. One such source was a group called the Samaritans. Phil later became an active member of this group, and he remains an operator and supporter of it. While at school Phil also honed his drumming skills by playing in the college-revue version of *Return to the Forbidden Planet*.

By the summer of 1990, Ed, Colin, and Phil had completed their degrees. They returned to Oxford to make a bit of money while waiting for Thom to rejoin them the next summer. At that point, they would all devote their energies to the band. Phil took jobs as an English teacher and a desk editor, while Ed became a barman and a photographer's assistant.

Colin, whose intellect is almost frightening, disappointed his mother (who had expected him to pursue an academic career) and did what seemed natural to him: he got a job at an Oxford record store. He wanted to expand his musical knowledge, and while he was criticized for his choice by most of the people he knew, he performed his job with pride. This would prove a blessing for the band.

In Exeter, Thom stayed with Headless for its two-year run, which netted one release and 30 gigs. Thom was writing songs with sHack, but at least one of these compositions — "High and Dry" — would not die with the college band. "The last live show we did was at Exeter's huge summer party," sHack says. He recalls that "part of our repertoire at the time was 'High and Dry,' but played at 1,000 miles an hour without any of the blissful emotion or subtlety of *The Bends* version."

As Thom reached the end of his term, he was still immersed in computer-manipulated art. Taking Michelangelo's Sistine Chapel painting, he changed the colors and called it his own. He obtained his degree, but was assured by his professors that he still couldn't paint.

So Thom's time at Exeter had drawn to a close. And the moment had come for Headless to be laid to rest. "It was always quietly asserted that [Thom's] loyalty was towards what he would call his 'Oxford band,'" explains sHack. "He seemed to have an agreement with his bandmates there that they would dedicate themselves to the project once they left college — it was like a pact . . . keeping everyone's parents happy by going to college, but always confident they would regroup for 'the big push' post studies. I was disappointed when he left Exeter, but at the time I would have been unable to commit to music full time, so it was expected."

"It was a real shame," continues sHack, "because we were on the verge of taking things more seriously, despite the fact that my own interest in dance music was beginning to eclipse my guitar-oriented upbringing." Yet Thom's departure from school didn't mean that he had quit town for good. "It was a sociocultural thing, as Thom understood implicitly. We used to throw and attend acid house parties around the time out on Dartmoor, and there never was a more liberal, excessive way of losing it. As a response to what we were hearing, even though Thom moved back [to Oxford], he was omnipresent in Exeter and would come and hang out in my techno-flat above the city. We'd spend days getting our heads around the basic electronic gear I had lying around, and John Matthias joined us to provide some strangely fucked-up violin work. We did our first show at a huge rave at the university doing Cubik-style tracks with Thom playing some textural guitar and doing a daft heavy-metal solo on one track."

This new project, which Thom would be a part of only briefly, was known as Flicker Noise. Thom played guitar and sHack acted as programmer and vocalist. But Thom only played the one show before deciding to devote himself exclusively to On a Friday. He just couldn't commit himself to Flicker Noise as well.

At home in Oxford, Thom and his friends attempted to take On a Friday to the next level by building up a hometown following. In a few short months, their lives would begin to change much faster than they could ever have expected.

NOTHING TOUCHES ME NOW

3

Aerial FX is a band that didn't really happen. Its members made an album and released a couple of singles, but to most of the world it never existed. This is the fate of most bands, to live and die in obscurity, and the stories of what becomes of a defunct band's members are usually left untold as well. Aerial FX may not generate much interest in the 1990s music scene — it has been compared to early Orchestral Manoeuvres in the Dark — but the two men who created this musical entity, Chris Hufford and Bryce Edge, have a story worth telling.

During the short life of the band, Hufford was vocalist, bassist, and guitarist, while Edge was keyboardist. The venture may have been unsuccessful, but it gave the two a feel for the music industry and some experience in production. And it gave them the confidence to establish Courtyard Studios in a small village near Abingdon in 1987. By 1990, facing financial troubles, the two were forced to reevaluate the endeavor. They sold off the studios then rented out space from the new owners so that they could continue to record bands.

The first great Hufford and Edge venture under this arrangement was working with a new Oxford outfit called Slowdive. This band spent much of 1991 in the studio working on the singles "Morning-rise" and "Holding Our Breath," and the full-length album *Just for a Day*, with Hufford serving as both engineer and producer. This time, Hufford and Edge managed to keep their heads above water, and the Slowdive releases generated a great deal of interest in their production skills.

Around the beginning of 1991, a young man named John Butcher visited the studio. In his pocket was a tape of fifteen songs made by a band that featured two of his former classmates at Abingdon, Thom Yorke and Colin Greenwood. It was the first recording by On a Friday.

Hufford's response was one of reserved interest. "There were some good tunes but it was all obviously ripped off mercilessly," he remembers. The final track stood out for him, though; he describes it as a "weird looped-up dance thing which was completely mental." Hufford was interested enough to ask for more (Irvin and Hoskyns).

By the summer of 1991, Thom had joined Ed, Colin, and Phil in the semidetached house they were sharing in Oxford. Thom had very little money, so he slept on the floor. This wasn't actually such a bad thing — the floor space he occupied was in the living room, where the quartet's massive music collection was kept. Putting time and money into building the collection seemed to have resulted in the neglect of housekeeping duties. "At first it was quite a nice house, but we turned it into a complete fucking hole," says Thom. "We'd just begun taking the band seriously, so there were musical instruments everywhere. We ripped half the wallpaper off taking the Hammond organ in and out. There was always fag ash everywhere. Plus, the carpet would roll down the stairs every time you went up them" (Collis, "Pulp").

The band members concocted some great stories about the house. The tenant before them had died dramatically, and they assumed she'd done so while in residence. They would find things in the house that had belonged to the deceased woman and spin wild tales about these artifacts. "One day we found this half eaten pork pie down the back of the sofa," recalls Colin. "It must've been there for months but you could still see the teeth marks. Of course, being morbid people we managed to convince ourselves that she'd choked on it" (Collis, "Pulp").

It wasn't long before Jonny moved in, too. The five musicians spent the year practicing, writing songs, and sitting around the house jamming. The band was now of paramount importance to them all. Soon after regrouping, they had decided to scrap the saxophone section. Jonny was shifted to guitar from keyboards, and as a result of tireless practice — and the fact that he was a very quick learner — he had begun to play like Queen's Brian May.

Thom would later say of writing new songs, "Having three guitarists [means] there's a lot of competition — who's going to come up with the best line first. Jonny always wins" (Morris). Jonny and Thom were writing a lot of songs, and soon they set their minds to recording demos. This new venture would require money; Thom's four track couldn't produce the professional quality they needed. Thom was holding down several jobs, but the most important to him was DJ-ing. He "spent all his money on records," reports Colin. "He used to make a fortune. He was a DJ . . . and he'd blow it all on crap records. He freely admits it. He has the worst record collection. Well, I think he was actually going for the bulk quantity over quality" (Bryan).

In Thom's unusual collection of music there were a few albums that helped to mold the sound of On a Friday. Jonny and Thom listened heavily to the Pixies (who during this year would release their final proper album, *Trompe le Monde*) and Lou Reed's *New York*. Both were drawn to certain American bands, especially those from the Boston area, like Throwing Muses and Buffalo Tom. These artists inspired Thom and Jonny to give their writing a harder edge.

The band finally made a new demo tape, this time using only three songs: "Give It Up," "What Is That You Say?" and the memorable "Stop Whispering." It was a good experience for them, but one bearing a price tag of over three hundred pounds. Thom and Colin's friend John Butcher once again took the tape out to Hufford's studios. This time their offer generated a better reaction. "These were great songs," Hufford declares. "Now they had an identity" (Irvin and Hoskyns).

Other songs they wrote during this period that became a part of On a Friday's roster were "Rattlesnake," "I Can't," and "Nothing Touches Me." Thom also wrote two tunes that dealt with life in Oxford — "Everybody Lies through Their Teeth" and "Jerusalem." Jonny later talked about a few of these tunes. "One track, 'Rattlesnake,' just had a drum loop that Thom did himself at home on a tape recorder with bad scratching over the top and kind of Prince vocals. 'The Chains' had viola and was meant to sound like The Waterboys. 'What Is That You Say?' was a feedback frenzy. After hearing it, I knew Thom was writing great songs and I knew what I wanted to do" (Doyle, "Party On").

Now, with the band in a more serious phase, it was time to get gigs. Their first post-university show was at a local club known as the Hollybush on 22 July 1991. The audience was six people strong, but the sparse attendance didn't bother On a Friday — it was a good chance for them to practice their live set. No pressure. Thom displayed a burning intensity that night, a trait that would become a band trademark.

Even though only half a dozen people had shown up, there was soon a buzz about the performance, and the band got a gig at the Jericho Tavern in August. Around this time, On a Friday began sending out letters to music journalists on its own letterhead inviting them to come out and see the band. Although they got no responses, they would soon grab the attention of the local paper, the *Curfew*.

At the Jericho show, the audience was only a bit larger than the one at the Hollybush, but Hufford turned up to see what the band was like as a live act. "I was completely and utterly blown away," he says. "Brilliant songs with the amazing power of the three guitars. I made a complete buffoon of myself, bursting backstage saying, 'I've got to work with you!' I was so excited by them. They had fantastic energy. I could see it on a world level, even then" (Irvin and Hoskyns). And so Hufford and Bryce arranged to work with On a Friday, to the benefit of both parties. On a Friday would help Hufford get his production studio off the ground, and the band would get professional-quality demos for only one hundred pounds each. The band members were elated about the arrangement and felt that they were now moving forward and upward.

The first order of business was to put out a recording for interested fans and to produce a demo the band could send off to record companies and clubs in an effort to get signed and line up gigs. They recorded five songs: "I Can't," which dealt with lack of confidence; "Nothing Touches Me," with its extremely catchy chorus; "Thinking about You"; "Phillipa Chicken"; and "You," definitely the strongest of the bunch. The recording was titled *Manic Hedgehog* after the local Oxford indie store, where it was sold for three pounds.

Meanwhile, Jonny had entered Oxford Polytechnic — also known as Oxford Brookes University — majoring in music and psychology. His tutor was an eccentric fellow who had enjoyed an extravagant lifestyle before going into teaching. He had been a member of a punk band in New York City and had lived with the legendary and very peculiar Iggy Pop for a time, so he fully understood Jonny's interests. When not immersed in his studies, Jonny practiced new songs by busking around Oxford with Thom, though this was more frustrating than helpful. They found that the best way to make money was to play REM covers, since by this time, the Athens, Georgia, band had become internationally famous. It was a very depressing period for the pair, but they do recall one shining moment when a couple of members of the local band Ride stood by and watched them play. Ride was then generating musical shockwaves with their unique, overpowering sound. It had put them at the forefront of the "shoe-gazing" movement, which was characterized by excessively loud guitar filled with reverb and drowned-out vocals. Most members of the bands in this scene would stare down at their shoes, or the stage, when they played live. But the Ride encounter wasn't enough to keep Jonny and Thom on the streets for long.

Colin was still at the Our Price record shop, and he couldn't have been better situated. There he met Keith Wozencroft, an EMI sales rep. Wozencroft had just attained a new position at EMI's head office: as artist-recruitment (A and R) person, he could sign new acts to the label. When he told Colin about his promotion, Colin reacted in the only sensible way. He handed Wozencroft one of the Manic Hedgehog tapes and said, "You should sign my band, then" (Irvin and Hoskyns).

Wozencroft didn't act as quickly as Colin might have liked, but he did show up to see the band at an open-air festival in Oxford. Despite the fact that the band played to an audience made up almost solely of girlfriends, Wozencroft was impressed. He asked the sound person to pass the word on to the boys that he had enjoyed the show and would keep in touch.

The other order of business that was weighing on the young musicians was the band's name. On a Friday might work for a group of kids who liked to practice on Fridays, but not for an established band. Besides, if the band was playing a gig on a day other than Friday, the show poster would read, "This Thursday: On a Friday." Not good. One suggestion that reflects the higher learning of the band's members was Jude, inspired by the Thomas Hardy novel *Jude the Obscure*, but they decided it was too pretentious . . . and obscure. Another, Thom's personal favorite, was Music, but his bandmates found it obnoxious. They also kicked around Gravitate, but ultimately rejected it. And so the name On a Friday stuck a little longer.

By October 1991, the band was getting a little more attention around town. They played another gig at the Jericho Tavern. Keith Wozencroft came back to hear them; his interest in the band was growing. On a Friday was the first group he took into his EMI/ Parlophone offices. His boss, EMI A and R director Nick Gatfield, who had been the sax player for Dexy's Midnight Runners, was also showing signs of interest.

People were talking about the intensity of the few gigs On a Friday had played. Word started to spread across England, and several other labels were taking notice. All this interest was palpable at the band's next Jericho Tavern show, held in early November, for which over twenty A and R people showed up. They'd been so anxious to get in that after the guest list filled up, they willingly paid at the door. Of this night Thom says, "There's no question we got lucky in the beginning, and that was the primary reason why the London music press didn't like us. It was ridiculous; the record companies were making outrageous offers and we had only maybe five songs, and this show that was exciting but sometimes haphazard as well" (Stoute, "Radiohead").

Of all the labels, EMI had the strongest presence at the show — company president Rupert Perry himself was there. And although the band had dropped his favorite song — "Phillipa Chicken" — from the live set, Perry was still enthusiastic. Nick Gatfield made an offer that night that the band was happy with. Chris Hufford and Bryce Edge, who had some contacts at EMI, agreed to manage the band. "Management had never been an ambition," says Hufford. "We'd always thought managers were complete tossers. But we'd learnt a lot. We thought, 'Let's be management where you put yourself in the artist's shoes.' We were naive about a lot of the business but we totally believed in the band" (Irvin and Hoskyns).

In December 1991, the band was in major-offensive mode. They were featured on the cover of the Oxford magazine *Curfew*, whose editor, Ronan, wrote that Thom "is possessed of that rare and special thing: a naturally musical singing voice." In the same article, an interview, Thom declared the band's strategy: "People sometimes say we take things too seriously, but it's the only way you'll get anywhere. We're not going to sit around and wait and just be happy if something turns up. We are ambitious. You have to be" (Ronan).

And so, after playing only eight gigs as On a Friday in 1991, the band sat down with the EMI people on 21 December to sign a record deal. The label offered to set up an imprint for the band that would appeal to indie enthusiasts, but On a Friday opted to become a part of the EMI team. Now that everything else was worked out and set down in writing, one issue started to preoccupy Wozencroft, Hufford, Gatfield, and the band members. What to do about that godawful name?

I AM BORN AGAIN

4

Armed with a record deal, the five young men from Oxford were ready to live out their dream of being pop stars. By 1992, they were already planning the release of their first EP, so if they were going to change their name they had to do it immediately. After a February gig at The Venue in Oxford, *Melody Maker*'s John Harris gave them an extremely favorable review, raving about the schizophrenic style of playing that marked the band's set. He concluded by remarking, "'Promising' seems something of an understatement." But Harris had one reservation: the band's name was "apt for beer-gutted pub rockers," not the crew he had witnessed (Harris, "Live!"). The band took the criticism to heart. Harking back to the 1986 Talking Heads' album *True Stories*, the quintet agreed to adopt the name of their favorite track, and in March 1992, Radiohead was born. Thom says that the name is "about the way you take information in. The way you respond to the environment you're put in" (*Radiohead: The Interview*).

As things accelerated, Jonny decided to leave school, and this led to tension between him and his mother. Colin explains, "She wasn't too concerned about me because I'd already got my degree but she thought our manager was the son of Satan for taking Jonny away from the first year of his music studies course at Oxford" (Stuart Clark). Jonny went to his tutor for advice. Recalling his own high times in the music industry, he encouraged Jonny to abandon his music/psychology studies after only one semester.

Still young, the five bandmates were not prepared for the fast pace of the music world. Things seemed to be happening much quicker than they had expected. Thom found himself turning to alcohol quite a bit in the early Radiohead days, drinking to excess like he had at Exeter. He also smoked a lot. Shaving his head, he created the first of the many new looks he'd adopt in the coming years. As the Radiohead enterprise started to eclipse all other concerns, the band members' personal priorities became distorted. "When we signed to EMI," says Colin, "we all made this decision where we thought the most important thing was the music . . . more important in some ways than qualities of friendship" (Mulligan).

The record company began to exert control: EMI execs felt the quintet should dress better; they insisted that they lacked style sense. This would have to be remedied. Colin reflects on this period of conflict: "When we started, our record company said, 'Oh boys, you need a stylist!' And we just said, 'No, no, we won't do it.'" They were given three hundred pounds to "get styled" — and only three hours in which to do it. "Phil is still wearing some of it," Thom said a few years later. "I threw all of mine away immediately. I bought bags and bags and bags of secondhand clothes and took them home and looked at them all" — and then he chose never to wear them (Mulligan). Colin approached the shopping excursion with a different, perhaps more practical, attitude. "I was still confused about what I wanted to do," he says, "and thought 'If [the band] ends I should get a suit so I can be looking strapped for the job interview" (Mulligan). Colin purchased a suit that he has never worn for a single Radiohead appearance.

And there was yet another obstacle: says Ed, "We once had this A and R man who said, 'Chaps, what you've gotta have is An Agenda. A manifesto'" (Nine, "Radio-Unfriendly Unit Shifters"). They had never thought of this, having naively gone into the industry for the music. Worried that an "agenda" was crucial to their success, they sat down and tried to work one out, but all they could muster was the determination to continue living in Oxford, despite the fact that success would come much faster if they relocated to London, the center of the music scene. It's unclear whether or not the agenda issue was actually important to EMI; the A and R man who had brought it up was fired two months later. "That's the fun," comments Colin — "spotting that nobody knows anything about how it all really works. But it's also the grief, when people pretend they know how things are going to go before it even has a chance to happen" (Nine, "Radio-Unfriendly Unit Shifters").

On 27 March 1992, the band was offered a major opening slot at The Venue in London with the Catherine Wheel and the God Machine. It was to be one of the very earliest gigs they played as Radiohead. And early that year Radiohead went back into the studio with Hufford and Bryce to make their first EP, *Drill*.

Radiohead in Oxford, 1992

"Not a clever move," is how Hufford now describes his direct involvement with the production of the EP. "A huge conflict of interest. I think Thom was very unsure of my involvement. I'd had that happen to me as an artist when one of our managers acted as producer — it was fine until we wanted to develop and move on — so I was acutely aware of what he was feeling, but I can be quite overbearing and opinionated in the studio" (Irvin and Hoskyns). Two songs had already been committed to tape, the original demos for "You" and "Thinking about You," part of the *Manic Hedgehog* offering. The EP also included "Stupid Car," and it opened with "Prove Yourself," a song dealing with suicide.

The release of *Drill* presented a few problems, which allowed the band even more insight into the kinds of mistakes that record companies can make. The EP was funded by EMI and released under the Parlophone imprint, but because the songs were taped before the band was signed and had originally been intended for an independent release, the recordings were fairly rough. The cover, designed by a company called Icon, was extremely expensive. Also, the first 3,000 copies of the EP were lost in the warehouse. *Drill* had to be pressed again, and this delayed its release. To make matters worse, a promotional copy of the EP was sent out to the press with a cover that read "Radiohead: *Drill*" even though the CDs inside were by Joe Cocker, another EMI artist (*Radiohead: The Interview*).

Drill was finally released on 5 May 1992, but it garnered very little interest, climbing no further than number 101 on the singles chart. Hufford and Edge decided it was time to step down as the band's producers. The reviews of the EP were not particularly favorable, but Radiohead noticed that critics rarely discussed their music, focusing instead on the fact that they had been signed very soon after forming (most journalists didn't know their history).

"After the EP came out and the slagging started, it made me so paranoid I wasn't able to write," admits Thom. "Everything I did seemed contrived because, true or not, I was anxious to avoid criticisms" (Stoute, "Radiohead"). Still, band members chose not to dwell on the bad press, since getting any attention at all was an achievement.

Like many new bands, Radiohead attempted to boost the single's sales by purchasing copies themselves, but this tactic failed miserably. "We all walked into a record shop in Nottingham the day the first single, the *Drill* EP, came out," remembers Colin. "We walked in, like 'Mmmm, I'll buy one of these.' The guy behind the counter said, 'Don't worry man, we'll give you one.' We said, 'No! We really want to buy one!' He said, 'Look, your record company's just given us 20 free ones and we can't shift them, not even for 99 [pence], so you might as well have a free one.' We were very depressed" ("Have You Ever . . . ," *Select* Jan. 1998).

Things started to look up for the band shortly after that when a friend told them that Gary Davies, the weekend-breakfast-show DJ for Radio 1, had featured "Prove Yourself" as the "Happening Track of the Week." Ears to the radio the following morning, all five musicians waited patiently and were ecstatic when Davies once again aired the single. Considering the relatively poor quality of the recording, this was a real achievement, and band members could speculate about how much more airplay their later, better-produced singles would get.

The band was also featured in a short *Melody Maker* interview conducted by John Harris, the first that could be read all over the world. In it, Thom articulated Radiohead's aims: "'Smells like Teen Spirit' had the kind of feel we're after. When it came on the radio, you had no choice but to listen to it. You couldn't just drive along and ignore it, it came out at you. I hope we'll come out of people's speakers in the same way." He also talked about the seriousness of the songs the band was writing and noted that "all songs come from a state of conflict" (Harris, "Totally Wireless").

Radiohead soon took to the road, playing a supporting role on the Catherine Wheel tour and joining another UK act, the Sultans of Ping, for several dates. The *Drill* tour took band members on the road for a month and a half before returning to the studio to record their next single. Of course, EMI had to draft a new production team. Nick Gatfield got in touch with American producers Paul Q. Kolderie and Sean Slade. After hearing "Stop Whispering," the two agreed to record Radiohead's next single. The band was excited at the prospect of working with them, as they had produced some of Radiohead's favorite artists, including Throwing Muses, Dinosaur Jr., and Buffalo Tom.

All the while, the British music scene was undergoing some major style shifts, which likely hindered Radiohead's early success in England. A new band called Suede was grabbing headlines all over the country with their Bowie-esque glam approach; fronted by Brett Anderson, the group had a stage presence that was incredibly captivating. Anderson swaggered across the stage spewing sexually ambiguous lyrics and copping an attitude that won over the British press. Suede was made for the press, with its extravagant personality, willingness to stir up controversy, and a sound that broke through the shoe-gazing style. The band was splashed on the covers of various music journals even before they had released their first single on Nude Records, "The Drowners," and were tagged the best new band in Britain. Over time, British music journalists would come to believe that Suede could do no wrong. Suede, they declared, would soon dominate the North American sound and go on to rule the music world.

Radiohead, trying to grab some audience and press attention for itself, was coming up empty-handed. One gig at a bar called Dudley JB's was possibly the most discouraging of their short tour, but — as they later learned — it was a difficult venue to play. "We walked onstage, there were about 50 people there, the bar was at one end and we were at the other," recalls Colin. "And everyone stayed at the bar. For the whole gig. At the end of the gig, this mad squaddie, who'd just gone AWOL, came into the dressing room and told us The Stone Roses had played there four times before they got any response" ("Have You Ever . . . ," *Select* Jan. 1998).

This dismal date behind them, Radiohead members headed off to Chipping Norton Studio in Oxford where they got down to work on their next EP with Kolderie and Slade. It was to be a double-A-side record with the tracks "Inside My Head" and "Million Dollar Question," songs that Thom had written about signing with a major label. The tracks were mediocre at best in the studio setting — though they had an incredible intensity when performed live — and the producers weren't impressed with what they had to work with.

While taking a break from recording, the band began playing around with another song that had made it into their live set during the Catherine Wheel tour. The track intrigued both Slade and Kolderie, but when they asked what it was Thom replied, "That's a Scott Walker song" (Irvin and Hoskyns). The two producers were disappointed that the best song this new band had in its roster was a Scott Walker cover, although, strangely, it wasn't one they recognized. As the recording session stretched well into the night with very little progress being made, Slade suggested the band play around with that Walker song again. Thom corrected him: he had not said "*a* Scott Walker song," but "*our* Scott Walker song." Delighted, the producers told the band to run through the number one more time. They didn't know as they were doing it that the song was being recorded. "At the end [of the song]," remembers Kolderie, "everyone in the place was silent for a moment and then they burst into applause. I'd never had that happen before" (Irvin and Hoskyns).

And so "Creep," based on an infatuation Thom had experienced in college, was captured on tape. It's ironic, given the response it elicited not only from the producers but also, in the coming months, from the rest of the world, that the band didn't really like the song. Jonny's grinding riff was one he normally used when tuning his guitar; when Thom heard it, he loved it and wanted to use it. Some contend that Jonny employed the riff deliberately to ruin the song, but Jonny also enriched the tune with a beautiful piano outro. Thom still didn't like the lyrics, but that didn't seem to matter. That night in the studio, Radiohead history was made. "Creep" would be the band's next single.

Some things move rapidly in the music business, but some things come painfully slow — this was the case with "Creep." The single was set for release, with "Inside My Head" and "Million Dollar Question" relegated to B-side status along with a simple yet powerful track titled "Lurgee." This last song, about breaking up but being better off for it, came out of a recording session during which Chris Hufford sat in the producer's chair.

The single was released on 21 September 1992 during a promotional tour that began at the end of August and saw the band provide support for various other acts. The EP was released on CD, cassette, and vinyl, and limited to only 6,000 copies per format. "Creep" debuted at number 78 before falling down, and then off, the British singles chart. This didn't surprise the band — Radio 1 had decided the song was too depressing for its listeners and only played it twice before taking it out of rotation.

To make the video for "Creep," the band revisited an Oxford club known as The Venue (formerly the Co-op Hall), where they had played before getting signed. The hall holds approximately four hundred people, but with all the wires and the video crew taking up space, only 250 people could be accommodated around the stage while the band played. The video, like the single, received little exposure in the UK.

Despite radio resistance, "Creep" was such a successful recording in the eyes of EMI that Kolderie and Slade remained at Chipping Norton Studio to record Radiohead's debut album. The challenge for both the producers and the band was that they had only three weeks to do it. The final product contained tracks recorded with eight guitar overdubs; this created a wall of sound and some noisy, distortion-induced music. Thom claims the band "hit the self-destruct button on all the pedals" in order to make "as much noise as we could" (Robbins). "It was a bit of a struggle," recalls Kolderie. "It was their first record and they wanted to be The Beatles, and the mix had to have no reverb, and they had all the ideas they'd ever come up with in twenty years of listening to records. But we managed to get it done" (Irvin and Hoskyns).

The band tried a few different things while in the studio, even though there was little time for experimentation. Jonny played guitar with a paintbrush on "Anyone Can Play Guitar," and at the end of the album's final track, "Blow Out," he scratched a coin up and down the edge of the guitar neck.

The album had a dry feel, as do most albums recorded live off the floor with limited production — usually the result of budget constraints. The effect was also evident on the Suede and PJ Harvey albums that were released in 1993. Radiohead and the production team played around with the mixes quite a bit, but usually reverted back to the original takes, and in the process the band became comfortable with the Trident, a mixing machine popular in recording studios during the 1970s. Thom says, "You can actually record anywhere, but it's mixing that is the important thing. You should mix quietly — people who mix their tracks at ear-splitting volume really don't have a clue. We go through an hour of mixing quietly, take a break, then come back to it and listen to it really fucking loud, then turn it back down again" (Doyle, "Cheap Thrills").

The album contained some wonderful tracks, including "Stop Whispering" and a new acoustic version of "Thinking about You." It also featured two songs recorded by Hufford at Courtyard Studios, "I Can't" and the "Creep" B-side "Lurgee." Band members, although generally pleased with the work of Kolderie and Slade, later admitted they preferred some of the Hufford versions of their songs to those executed by their new production team.

In the studio the musicians tried to make things more interesting. They used Phil as a means of intimidation, jokingly referring to him as "Mad Dog." The producers were warned that if Mad Dog were to get angry he'd heave his drums out the window. Kolderie and Slade went to master the album at Fort Apache studios in Boston, far away from the crazed percussionist.

On the road, the band opened for the Irish pop group the Frank and Walters, whose EPS had won quite a bit of attention from the music press and who were constantly on tour. This quality — a compulsion to work hard — had attracted Radiohead to many of the bands that they played with. They wanted to find acts that were as interested in self-promotion as they were.

By the latter part of 1992, the band noticed that something had changed in their live gigs. The audience was singing along with certain songs, notably "Prove Yourself," and in particular the line "I'm better off dead." Given that Thom's songs were very personal, written as a form of therapy, he found this quite weird. Still, it was encouraging to know their music was finally sending out feelers. As the end of the year approached, Radiohead embarked on yet another tour; they were on the road continuously from the end of August until December supporting Kingmaker, a young new band that had met with early success through its Wonderstuff-style album *Eat Yourself Whole*. Unfortunately for Radiohead, they weren't actually opening for Kingmaker, but for a juggler who warmed up for Kingmaker. Not exactly a career high point.

While on the Kingmaker tour Thom wrote a new song, which he taped. Titled "Nice Dream," it was an intriguing composition, and the rest of the band loved it. Another song written right after the recording of the debut album was "The Bends," and over the coming weeks and months Radiohead would write still more songs, even though their debut album hadn't even been released.

At one of the December shows, *New Musical Express* journalist Keith Cameron put in an appearance. He later gave Radiohead its worst press to date. Reviewing one of the band's first headlining appearances — at the Smashed Club in London — Cameron concluded with the line: "Radiohead are a pitiful, lily-livered excuse for a rock 'n' roll group" (Cameron, "Live"). And above the caption "Uglee — Oh Yeah!" was a photo of Thom. Although the band tried not to take bad press too seriously, these words had a painful resonance. The band's relationship with the British press began to disintegrate, and would continue to do so for years. (Surprisingly, *New Musical Express* included "Creep" in their top-ten-singles list that year.)

Again, Radiohead members just had to grit their teeth and move on. There were still a few unfinished matters to take care of concerning their debut album. A title, for one. This is how an apt title was finally found: Hufford came to the band one day with a bootleg tape by the American group the Jerky Boys. To create material for their recordings, the boys would cold call people at their homes or workplaces and ask them bizarre questions or pretend to know them. Such tactics freaked out the person being called, but provided plenty of entertainment for the Jerky Boys and their following, which included members of an Oxford shoe-gazing act known as Chapterhouse. On a visit to the United States, Chapterhouse had obtained the tape that Hufford played for Radiohead. The band was fascinated. What the Jerky Boys were doing was sick — there was a lot of twisted sexual content — but the whole undertaking was still very interesting. "The notion of phoning people up cold is so '90s," says Thom. "It's just the ultimate sacrilege — turn up in someone's life and they can't do anything about it" (Cavanagh). One track features a Jerky Boy calling a man and acting like his mother, opening the conversation by saying "Pablo, honey." He then begs the so-called Pablo to come to Florida; the man hangs up. "'Pablo Honey' was appropriate for us," explains Thom, "being all mother's boys" (Cavanagh). This notion of being mama's boys derives from the fact that the members of Radiohead came from nice, middle-class homes and had been provided with good educations. They didn't have the wild, unstable upbringings common to many of their colleagues in the music business.

At the beginning of 1993, after less than a month's break from touring, the band headed back onto the road. From 13 January to the beginning of March, they promoted their forthcoming releases — a third single and the debut album. "Anyone Can Play Guitar" hit the shelves on 1 February, and the band finally entered the top 40, debuting at number 32. The single grabbed a bit of attention due to the line it contained about Jim Morrison, written after Thom saw the movie *The Doors*. Receiving a good dose of positive press, "Anyone Can Play Guitar" was even named single of the week in *Melody Maker*. The release's lead track was backed by two songs produced and engineered by James Warren and Chris Hufford, "Faithless, The Wonder Boy" and "Coke Babies."

Only three weeks after the EP came out, *Pablo Honey* appeared in record shops. Reviews of the album were fair, with most journalists giving it a passing grade. *Select* magazine's Steve Lamacq summed up Radiohead's unique sound perfectly by saying, "They roam through shoe-gazing and punk and end up in bed with . . . none of them." The album debuted on the British charts at number 25, the highest position the band had ever achieved. Along with twelve diverse and wonderful tracks, the album also featured an eye-opening cover — a baby inside a sunflower. Thom had chosen the baby photo because he thought the infant resembled him.

The back cover of the album, as Colin explains, is "the body of Jesus Christ floating over the Las Vegas strip. It's all deep and meaningful. I don't know what it means. [It was] done by this mad woman with red hair in England called Lisa Bunny Jones, whose mother takes her to hardcore thrash concerts" (Bryant). Inside the sleeve there's a band photo taken during the "Anyone Can Play Guitar" video shoot, and the large photo in the middle of the insert was shot at the bottom of an empty swimming pool. Band members laughed at the fact that in the picture Jonny's head is down so low that his hair blends in with his shirt, making him appear headless. During autograph sessions, they would often draw his head back on. The CD sleeve also includes a picture of a live iguana and a plastic alligator, referred to by the band as Arnold and Gordon, respectively (Bryant).

Now that their new album was being released around the world, it was finally time for Radiohead to launch a promotional invasion of other countries. They headed off to Israel at the end of March, unaware of what was waiting for them. In Tel Aviv, "Creep" had already broken and hit. It was the first city in the world to fall for the release, but it would not be the last. Radiohead played a few gigs in Tel Aviv, did several interviews, and returned to England where they put out what would be their last single for quite some time: the nonalbum track "Pop Is Dead," originally set for inclusion on *Pablo Honey*. The song, an "epitaph to 1992," was accompanied by three more tracks, all live: "Banana Co." was recorded at a session set up for Signal Radio in Cheshire; "Creep" and "Ripcord" came from a show the band did at London's Town and Country Club on 14 March (Paphides). The reviews of the single were poor at best, and the band was criticized for exploiting "Creep" — now a fairly well-known song in Britain — by using it on a B-side, even though it was a different version.

The single only made it to number 42 before slipping off the charts, and the songs received little radio play. Still, the band didn't lose hope. Regardless of this lack of attention — Suede and the Auteurs were grabbing all the indie press — Thom remained determined: "I want nothing more in the whole world than to be a star" (Collins). Hufford knew the band had the potential for greater success, but for the time being he was content with their position in the music world. He decided that Radiohead should only do a short tour for *Pablo Honey* before beginning work on a second album. Says Hufford, "A giant leap isn't actually healthy for a band; it needs to grow and understand naturally how things work" (Irvin and Hoskyns).

WHAT THE HELL AM I DOING HERE?

5

San Francisco radio station 106.9 KROQ wields a phenomenal influence over the American music scene. It has built a reputation for being the first to air new and unknown bands. Songs played initially on KROQ often make their way onto the playlists of other radio stations across the country. The station is renowned not only for introducing bands, but also for making them household names. Making them stars.

A tape of *Pablo Honey* fell into the hands of KROQ DJs. But, unlike the record spinners at Radio 1 in Britain, the KROQ jockeys could see right away that "Creep" was exceptional and bound for glory. Thanks to the influence of the likes of Nirvana and Pearl Jam, personal songs that reflected a sense of self-loathing were just what American kids were craving. However, there was a censorship issue to overcome first. In the buildup to the chorus of "Creep," Thom sings, "You're so fucking special"; KROQ knew it wouldn't be able to get away with that. Station reps contacted Capitol Records in the United States (which was in charge of all EMI releases) and arranged for a touched-up version of the song. By March, the sanitized "Creep" had hit American radio, and it quickly made it into regular rotation.

Pablo Honey was released in the United States in mid-April. It soon made its way onto *Billboard*'s top 200 charts. It rose slowly as American interest in Radiohead grew. In June, when "Creep" was released in America as a single, it shot up the *Modern Rock* charts to number two — an incredible showing, especially since the band had yet to cross the ocean. The single then hit number 34 on the *Hot 100 Singles* chart, another coup for such a new band.

At the beginning of May, Radiohead wrapped up its tour of England

and prepared to penetrate other countries. Beginning with Ireland, the band then hit Denmark, Sweden, Holland, and, finally France, where Thom debuted two new songs, "Bullet Proof" and "Lozenge of Love," at an acoustic showcase. The band's overall plan was to sell 20,000 to 30,000 albums to keep the record company happy. They hoped, also, to return to the studio with a new repertoire of songs to record by the end of 1993.

But the next order of business was to tour the United States and do two television performances. The first of these was on Arsenio Hall's popular late-night talk show. The influential Hall introduced Radiohead as one of the most exciting new acts around. Wearing a yellow raincoat, Thom delivered a stunning rendition of "Creep." Soon afterwards, the band was featured on *Late Night with Conan O' Brien*. Again, the performance was memorable, and the song tapped an even wider audience. Aside from doing these television spots, the band spent its first few days in the United States talking to the press, often working for over sixteen hours straight. Whether the five musicians were prepared for it or not, they were in the process of becoming rock stars — at least in the United States.

Most of Radiohead's shows — mainly headlining gigs — were sold out, some in record time. Band members were chauffeured around the different cities they visited in limousines, and it was not unusual for Thom to wake up in the morning in his hotel room, turn on MTV, and see his own image on video; the "Creep" clip was by this time in light-medium rotation.

All five Radiohead members were surprised by their success. And thrilled. Although inherently modest, they didn't feel like shying away from it all, and so found themselves struggling with their new popularity. "If you say you want to be desperately successful, people don't like that," remarks Thom. "Everyone in Britain's obsessed with credibility, trying to look like you're not selling records when you are" (Robbins).

While in Chicago at the end of June the band heard the final version of "Stop Whispering," which had been remixed by Chris Sheldon. This new mix was overlaid with strings; while very different from the *Pablo Honey* version, it was still remarkably strong. But the band worried that with the release of a second single their promotion of the album would be prolonged until after Christmas, and they were eager to get to work on their second album. Said Thom: "It's starting to get a bit frustrating for us because we've got twenty or thirty songs ready to go into rehearsal, and we just want to start working on that to get a better perspective of what we're doing now" (Bryant).

A passionate and heated performance
at one of the many *Pablo Honey* shows

Although the album was only a few months old, Radiohead had been on the road almost continuously since January of 1992, and the pressures of touring were beginning to take their toll. Still, band members were able to retain their sense of humor. They had a great laugh on 2 July during their Toronto debut at Edgefest, a gig many considered their weirdest to date. They performed on the Ontario Place Forum's revolving stage; the audience was situated all around the stage in stands and on the lawn. The band likened the experience to playing Disneyland, and, "For some silly reason," said Thom, "the fact that people would be able to see our bums put us into fits of laughter" (Stoute, "Radiohead").

At about this time the band received its best review yet. Now they felt they had truly made it. The popular animated MTV show *Beavis and Butthead* — featuring two moronic and morally bankrupt kids who spend most of their time watching and criticizing music videos — played "Creep." Butthead expressed utter disdain for the song, but Beavis assured him it would get better. When Jonny did his riff leading into the chorus, Butthead finally got into it. "It's so cool to get on a programme like *Beavis and Butthead*," says Thom. "That was great. My favourite bit is where Beavis goes, 'If they didn't have that bit in the song that sucked, then the other bit wouldn't be so great.' Yes!" Talking about Beavis, Thom cracks: "He should write for the music press" (McLean, "Radiohead"). And Jonny, reflecting on Beavis's excitement during the chorus, says: "He nearly cums, doesn't he?" (Considine).

Not only were Beavis and Butthead singing the praises of the band, but also Michael O'Neil, production assistant for MTV, was cheering them on. "They know how to write songs, they know how to sing and they know how to play. They're cred. They've got attitude. They're alternative crossover! They're like Jim Morrison-meets-Jimi Hendrix. MTV love them. They're rockin' the country" (Lester).

While the MTV/*Beavis and Butthead* promotions may have seemed harmless and funny, Radiohead's managers and producers began to realize that "Creep" was overshadowing the success of the album, which was a strong collection of twelve songs, each powerful in its own right.

Capitol Records was "doing 'I'm a Creep' contests and placing ads that said 'Beavis and Butthead Say They Don't Suck,'" points out Kolderie. "I remember Bryce saying, 'This is horrible, it's looking like a one-hit wonder unless we can save this baby'" (Irvin and Hoskyns). It was becoming ridiculous. The band played a few songs — including

"Creep" — at an MTV *Beach Party* show, which was videotaped. The station then began to air this live-performance version of "Creep" as a brand-new video. "We swore that would be the last time we'd do that fucking thing," says Thom (Considine).

"Creep" was also affecting the band's image. And, as Jonny comments, "the irony [wasn't] lost on people. All these gorgeous, bikinied girls shaking their mammary glands, and we're playing 'Creep' and looking horrible" (Considine). Radiohead's members were becoming sex symbols. Both Thom and Jonny modeled for fashion-magazine spreads. Thom also underwent various hair transformations throughout the 1993—94 tour. He even had blonde extensions done — instant long hair for the United States visit. "My image changes were a result of a low boredom threshold and a lack of confidence in what I look like," he admits (Doyle, "New").

Whatever individual band members felt about their looks, Radiohead was featured in the American teen mag *Sassy* under the heading "Cute Boys, Loud Guitars." Still, the irony that all this adulation had been generated by "Creep," a song about lacking personal confidence, seemed to escape almost everyone.

While the band could take a lot of this promotional activity lightly, one interpretation of the song surfaced that could not be laughed off. Thom received a shocking letter from a prison inmate that read, "I'm the creep in that song. I killed this bloke. They made me do it. It wasn't me, it was the words in my head." Thom was shaken: "I felt like someone had walked over my grave" (Wiederhorn, "Radiohead").

There were also the letters from fans who believed Thom knew the answers to their problems. And soon, of course, band members had to deal with a traditional rock-and-roll phenomenon: groupies. While they were in Los Angeles, where they played two sold-out gigs, a naked girl positioned herself outside Jonny's hotel-room door, hoping to shag the young guitarist. She was disappointed. "There's a hidden rule that no one goes with groupies," explains Ed. "I hate that side of things, it's so dirty and seedy. It might be alright in a Guns N' Roses video, but it's not for us. We're quite a moral band, you know" (Lestor).

Though the press was fascinated by the enigmatic Thom, journalists weren't always as flattering as he might have liked, and he learned to keep them at arm's length. He came to realize that despite the very personal nature of his songs he didn't owe anyone an explanation. "[I did this] interview in America when this woman just said, 'Tell me about your childhood — were you a fucked up kid?'" recalls

Thom. "I just sat there for five minutes and decided not to answer her. And I haven't said anything on the subject since. Once I've given people that information, I find it very, very painful" (Harris, "Radiohead").

During interview sessions, band members came off as bridge-playing, tea-drinking British lads, very thoughtful and courteous. And while this may simply have been them being themselves, it was also kind of a comic performance — one that was taken quite seriously by their interviewers.

The promotion work continued on into the summer, and the album was becoming even more successful in the United States. But now powerful Capitol Records — not the band — was in the driver's seat. Capitol was very serious about increasing Radiohead's sales in the United States. Company brass believed that "Creep" was a perfect fit for a popular market niche. "It's an exceptional song," maintained Bruce Kirkland, Capitol's general manager/senior vice president of marketing. "It was the right track at the right time. Our goal is to add to the situation. . . . We want to really establish the act now. We're releasing a great follow-up track, and we're going to keep them on the road" (Barzillo).

The "follow-up track" that Kirkland referred to was "Stop Whispering." Although Thom wasn't too keen on releasing it, the single came out in the United States later that year. It entered the *Modern Rock* charts at number 23, but immediately fell off. American fans didn't care about other songs that Radiohead had to offer; they were quite satisfied with "Creep," the teen-angst summer anthem.

In their live shows, the band tried to fight this obsession, moving "Creep" around in the set list (it was never the closing song) in an effort to spark interest in other album tracks. Sadly, it didn't seem to work. "I remember on the 'Creep' tour we used to get people that would come and just leave after 'Creep,' and we'd sort of stop them afterwards and ask them why," Jonny told me. "And they would say, 'Oh we saw you on MTV,' and they were the type to go and see Nirvana and leave after 'Smells like Teen Spirit.' There is like this core audience that just goes to see the songs that they have seen the videos for. It's quite bizarre."

The UK press was still not showing an interest, apparently concluding that Radiohead wouldn't last as the outfit had only one thing going for it: "Creep." The song had become an albatross. The Radiohead show at the Academy in New York City was reviewed by Jon Wiederhorn for *Melody Maker*. Wiederhorn not only slagged the band for its success in the United States, but also closed his review by saying, "Creeps of the world unite. At least for now" (Wiederhorn, "Live!"). "About the worst thing they said was that not only was Radiohead a one-hit wonder," says Colin, "but the band would never evolve past 'Creep.' If you listen to *Pablo Honey* with an open mind, you'll see that 'Creep' isn't representative of the direction of the band" (Howell). Jonny also discusses the bad press the band received in Britain: "There's a bit of a double standard in the British press. On one hand there's a lot of pressure to do well in America and on the other hand, there's the attitude your music must be really stupid if it does well there" (Tourangeau). This entrenched paradoxical attitude would prove hard to shake.

Radiohead's tour of the United States finally ended in the middle of July, and then MTV began airing the *Beach Party* version of the "Creep" video. Its success catapulted *Pablo Honey* to number 32 on *Billboard*'s top 200 albums chart in the first week of August, and it remained at those heights until mid-September. With the increase in sales this triggered, Capitol expected the band to return to the United States in the near future. Radiohead was already set to come back in the middle of September to tour with Belly until early November, but Capitol urged them to take an opening slot in the upcoming Duran Duran tour. The band resisted the pressure, sticking with their original plan.

Back in Europe, Radiohead played a few festivals in Belgium and Holland before preparing for their performance at England's annual Reading Festival. They knew a powerful showing at this major musical event would prove the British press wrong and give them the opportunity to make some inroads with the lackluster British audience. But luck just wasn't with them. Neither was good health. Hours before this key gig, Radiohead pulled out. Thom recalls the day: "The morning of the Reading gig I couldn't say anything and Rachel, my girlfriend, was on the phone ringing up our manager saying, 'He can't speak!' I'm fully aware that the reason a lot of people thought we didn't do Reading was that I was too shit-scared. And I'm sure that part of it was that I was so scared that my voice just collapsed. I went to see a Harley Street specialist the next week and he felt my neck and it was just like concrete" (Bailie, "Go Wired").

In absolute misery, Thom responded the way he often did when confronting his own limitations: he sat down and wrote a song. The end product was the vitriolic "My Iron Lung." The song is "more a statement about some of the people who come to see us," he says. "Or, certain members of certain audiences we've experienced. They haven't really got beyond toilet training as far as I can see. Not really our audience" (Nine, "Radio-Unfriendly Unit Shifters"). "My Iron Lung" contained a soon-to-be-famous line: "This is our new song / Just like the last one / A total waste of time." While it wouldn't be released or included in the band's live set for awhile, the song would soon be heard by many.

At home in Oxford, band members had little time to enjoy their us triumph — first, because their home country really didn't care about them much, and second, because the sheer effort they needed to expend in order to make it in other parts of the world was taking a physical toll on them. Facing a British press that was indifferent at best, hostile at worst, the five musicians struggled to maintain their sense of humor: Phil's pet parrot, Bert, a highly intelligent bird, had listened to *Pablo Honey* so often that he could now sing all of the tracks; Phil joked that Bert's versions were better.

Before departing for their second us tour, the band got a modest but much-needed boost from British music fans. The reissue of "Creep" was released on 6 September, and it debuted at number seven, Radiohead's best showing on the charts to date. It was even named single of the week by *Melody Maker*. For obvious reasons, Radiohead hadn't been keen on reissuing the single, but the record company insisted that it was a good idea, especially given the fact that so few of the original had been pressed. It was released on both cd and vinyl, and featured one new B-side: "Yes I Am." Of course, Radiohead still had to take some flak: the vinyl EP opened with an acoustic version of "Creep," recorded for KROQ, and the band (as they had anticipated) was criticized for putting out a third version of the song.

Radiohead met up with Belly in America, and the tour got under-way. While it was not a particularly great period for the band, they were in for a pleasant surprise when they reached Athens, Georgia. The stage at the venue that had been booked for the evening's gig was actually sinking into the ground, and so the show was relocated to the 40 Watt Club. There the boys of Radiohead met members of REM, a band that had been a powerful inspiration for them.

"[Michael] Stipe was a huge influence," explains Thom. "I thought, 'Who is this guy rambling on and on and I can't make out any of the words?' I want to do that" (Muretich).

"Peter Buck said recently in an interview that if, in your career, you write three songs that people go crazy about all over the world, so that everyone knows them wherever you go — then you've done what you set out to do," says Thom. "I read that and thought, 'Yeah!'" (Jennings, "Creepshow"). What Buck failed to explain was how to tour the world successfully on the basis of one hit single while remaining in good spiritual and physical shape. The health of Radiohead's members was deteriorating, and there seemed to be no simple solutions to the problem. "I was just sick all the time, like losing my voice," Thom recalls. "And my back went out. There was one particular time when I got off the bus in San Francisco and just collapsed on the ground" (Ross).

There were a few bright moments. One occurred on 13 October in New York City, when Radiohead received a gold record for US sales of *Pablo Honey*. Among the first congratulations they received was a fax from another British band, Suede. Their impulse was a generous one, considering the fact that Suede had been unable to match Radiohead's US sales.

But as the tour continued, band members' spirits deteriorated. The fun that had at one time been their fundamental reason for playing together had disappeared, and they had become fed up with one another. Not only was the arduous tour schedule dragging them down, but they were also wild with frustration at the fact that they had new songs but couldn't record them. "We joined this band to write songs and be musicians, but we just spent a year being a juke box instead," complained Jonny (McLean, "Radiohead"). The five musicians began working on new material during sound checks. They added "Nice Dream" to their live set, complementing "The Bends," which they'd been playing for most of the year.

The tour with Belly almost led to Radiohead's demise, but they somehow held on, even though upon completion of that US tour they were committed to a month-long slot opening for James in Europe. Only then would they get their break. Before leaving the US, the band played what they were told would be their most important gig yet. Canceling other engagements to make room on their calendar, they flew to Las Vegas, where they were slated to open for fellow countrymen Tears for Fears. The evening started very early, so when Radiohead took the stage the audience was still sparse. The promise of reaching a potential new following evaporated. To top things off, roadies for the popular 1980s act were nasty to Radiohead. Revenge was in order. Recalls Thom: "[The lights were] down the front and they were all eminently kickable. We smashed them all in and it was great." When Tears for Fears took the stage, Roland Orzabal expressed his enthusiasm for Radiohead by doing a cover of "Creep" as an encore. He completely missed the point of the song. "It was Vegas and over-the-top and cabaret," recalls Ed. "He changed the lyrics saying he was special," Colin adds. "And there was no self-doubt in the tone of his voice" (Doyle, "Party On").

The tour finally came to an end with a couple of Canadian dates, and the band flew off to Germany to support James. While this would prolong the band's road time — and thus further erode their health and add to their misery — it was a chance for them to play large venues in Europe. They also got to play at the G-Mex in Manchester, James's hometown — a very important gig to be a part of. As soon as the tour concluded, Radiohead went home for a six-week break. "When I got back to Oxford, I was unbearable," recalls Thom. "You start to believe you're this sensitive artist who has to be alone, this melodramatic, tortured person, in order to create wonderful music" (Thompson).

This was also a time of reflection for the band, but what they saw left them wondering what they'd really accomplished over the previous two years. They may have sold over a million copies of *Pablo Honey,* but most audiences just couldn't see beyond "Creep." "We didn't feel like it was a successful album," explains Jonny. "It had a successful song, but it wasn't a successful album" (Brown).

Radiohead had to look forward. They knew they had much better songs waiting to be recorded. "The second album is going to be much better than the first," Thom said confidently. "The first one was quite flawed, and hopefully the new one will make more sense. I like the first album, but we were very naive. We didn't really know how to use the studio" (Jennings, "Creepshow"). Colin also speculated about what the future might hold: "I think that within Radiohead's school of guitar noise, there's a mid-tempo acoustic-ballads band struggling to get out. If we record enough albums and we're secure enough, perhaps we'll do a Neil Young 'Harvest' album" (Robbins). Summing up, Thom declared: "It's going to be a lot calmer and a lot simpler, without being boring. The hysteria will be subtle" (Jennings, "Creepshow").

WHERE DO WE GO FROM HERE?

6

One of the most important producers in the music world is John Leckie. It's surprising that more bands don't break down his door trying to get him to listen to their songs, to offer a word of advice. After all, Leckie has worked relentlessly over the past three decades to learn everything there is to know about the inner workings of a studio.

Starting out in the early 1970s, Leckie got a job at Abbey Road Studios as tape operator. His earliest work was on the George Harrison album *All Things Must Pass*. He was soon assisting the other Beatles with their various solo projects, including *Plastic Ono Band 1* by John Lennon and Yoko Ono. Over the next few years, Leckie moved on from being a tape operator to become an engineer and mixer of various albums, including Pink Floyd's *Dark Side of the Moon* and *Wish You Were Here*, as well as Mott the Hoople's highly acclaimed *Mott*. Soon Leckie was in the producer's chair, working on XTC's sophomore single, the *3D EP*, and the band's debut album, *White Music*. When EMI stipulated in 1978 that Abbey Road employees had to work exclusively with EMI artists, and only in that prestigious studio, Leckie decided to go freelance. He valued the bonds he had forged with many bands not signed to EMI (Brannin and Gimbel).

Continuing to work with XTC, Leckie also produced Magazine's *Real Life*, an album that Susan Greenwood would later buy and play for her younger brothers. Throughout the 1980s, Leckie worked on numerous albums by Mark E. Smith's influential band the Fall. He also produced the Stone Roses' revolutionary self-titled 1988 debut. Later Leckie would work with an eclectic array of artists, including Robyn Hitchcock and the New Egyptians, the Verve, and Denim. He worked on the Stone Roses' follow-up album, but as the weeks turned into months, and the months into years — four, to be exact — Leckie backed out of the unfinished project.

In 1993, while Leckie was working with the very popular Oxford outfit Ride, someone sent him *Pablo Honey* and some demos that Radiohead had made while in the studio. He had previously shown interest in working with the band after hearing some of their songs. Both parties hoped to work together on the follow-up album, which the band wanted to begin that year. However, Leckie was tied up with Ride through the year, and Radiohead had tour commitments, so both producer and band had to wait until 1994 to connect.

At the end of February, Radiohead and Leckie converged at RAK Studios in London. While happy that Radiohead had found universal success with "Creep," EMI now expected the band to surmount their one-hit-wonder status. They needed an equally great song that would appeal to people all over the world. In short, EMI was telling Radiohead to go write another hit.

That pressure from EMI plus the band's relative inexperience in the studio (recall that *Pablo Honey* only took three weeks to make) was a recipe for failure. Everyone sat around the studio and tried out new things, but they came up with nothing. All five band members were unhappy with what they were doing; they couldn't work under such duress. "If you're starting off an album trying to record four hit singles, everyone gets a bit twitchy and you begin to question everything," explains Leckie. "It kind of affected the first few weeks of recording because every three or four days the record company or manager would turn up to hear these hit singles, and all we'd done was got a drum sound or something" (Doyle, "Diary").

Attempting to describe this impasse, Colin explains that it "wasn't creative block at all; Thom and Jonny are very prolific and we had the tunes. What we got bogged down on was finding a direction. Obviously we had to get as far away from 'Creep' as possible. How to do that became this huge energy-sucking black hole" (Howell). Says Thom, "We really had nothing we could use at all. We were paranoid and everything came out wrong. We were totally anal — to use an American saying" (Monk).

John Leckie was beginning to look like the most unlucky producer in Britain. Emerging from a four-year stint with the Stone Roses, he appeared to have taken a wrong turn and hit a brick wall. But while Radiohead was confused and unhappy with what was going on in the studio, Leckie never tried to take over the sessions, opting instead to let band members work things out for themselves, answer their own questions, and decide how best to record their songs. Ed maintains that was "very good in the sense that he gave us scope to discover our confidence; he wasn't going to lead us" (Baily).

What did get to Leckie, however, were some of the demands coming from the record company. "There was a lot of 'Jonny's got to have a really special sound,'" he explains. "I said, 'He's got one already,' but we spent days hiring in different amplifiers and weird guitars for him. In the end he used what he'd been using for the last couple of years and I just recorded it straight" (Irvin and Hoskyns).

The first session lasted a little over two months, and very little was accomplished. The first satisfying recording that came out of these sessions was "Just," but the song needed rigorous editing — in its original form, it clocked in at over seven minutes. The band also tried to fulfill the record company's wishes by recording four possible hits: from their set list they chose "The Bends," "Killer Cars," "Nice Dream," and "Sulk." Leckie went to Abbey Road Studios to mix these tracks while the band continued working on other material. Left alone, they practiced "Black Star" for an hour, then recorded it. It stands as the only song on the album produced by Radiohead, with the help of Leckie's engineer, Nigel Godrich.

One song was actually written in the studio — "Planet Xerox." Then, realizing that Xerox was a trademark, they changed the title to "Planet Telex." After Thom and Jonny had worked out the chorus, the band decided to go out for a night of drinking before recording the track. When they returned, Jonny went off to bed while Ed, Thom, and John Leckie worked on the piano portion (with Thom manning the keys) before getting the vocals down. "I remember when Thom was recording 'Planet Telex,'" says Colin. "It was about 2 or 3 A.M., and he was lying on his back on the floor. I was watching television, thinking, 'What is this?' It sounded really tedious. But then it all came together quite beautifully" (Baimbridge). Adds Thom, "Ed remembers it more, but apparently I sang it all with my head on the floor because I couldn't stand up. I was bent double and I hadn't a clue what I was singing" (Malins, "Scuba Do").

They added a drum loop to the track, and produced another layer by playing around with the outro on the original version of "Killer Cars" with a Mac Soundtool. Over the course of the year, this song would be remixed by various DJs and producers to create versions that were used as B-sides on singles from the new album.

By the end of March, the record company had decided to delay releasing a single from the album, so the epic recording session continued with everyone feeling a bit less pressured. Leckie, while giving

65

the band free rein, stuck to the recording style he had established, which meant laying down most of the guitar parts first to give the vocals a guide. Soon the tracks started coming a bit easier, including the song that had Thom introduced the band to in late 1992, "Nice Dream." It had since gone through some transformations; throughout 1993, he had worked on the lyrics, and they were now much better. The guitar outro was accompanied by sounds from the Arctic, furnished by Leckie from a tape he had in his collection.

One of the most frustrating songs for the band was "Fake Plastic Trees." The musicians found it impossible to capture a satisfying performance of the song, and soon began trying Leckie's patience. After playing around with it at Abbey Road for awhile, they decided to take a short break and attend a Jeff Buckley gig. The American singer/songwriter turned out to be an inspiration. "[Buckley] just had a Telecaster and a pint of Guinness and it was just fucking amazing," recalls Colin. "Then we went back to the studio and tried an acoustic version of 'Fake Plastic Trees.' Thom sat down and played it in three takes, then burst into tears afterwards. And that's what we used for the record" (Dalton). Radiohead wanted to add a background of strings to the track, so Leckie recruited Caroline Lavelle, a professional cellist who had played with Peter Gabriel. The band brought in Johnny Matthias, who had played with Thom and sHack in Exeter. It may have seemed odd to blend the skills of an amateur and a professional on the same track, but the results were beautiful. Jonny rounded things out by playing the studio's Hammond organ on the track — the same one that John Lennon had used. Everyone was proud of the end product.

"Street Spirit," written like "My Iron Lung," in the summer of 1993, and incorporating a difficult arpeggio executed perfectly by Ed, was also laid down during this productive period. The final result left them all speechless. By May, the sessions were still not completed, but the band had touring obligations in the Far East and Australia, preceded by a few shows in England. So, despite the fact that they were on a minor roll in the studio, Radiohead had to return to the road to promote *Pablo Honey* some more.

Two nights before the band's show at the Astoria in London, Thom sprained his ankle while playing "Anyone Can Play Guitar." As it turned out, he had a greenstick (or partial) fracture, and so the band soldiered on, not missing a show. At the Astoria gig, which was videotaped for release later in the year, Leckie set up recording equipment with the hope of capturing a decent live version of "My Iron Lung," a track that was not coming together in the studio. The live Astoria version is actually the one that made it onto the album, though Thom had to add vocals to the track later on.

Then it was off to Japan, where the band had developed a strong following. Here, quite a few Radiohead pressings had been (and would continue to be) released that would eventually be considered collectors' items. In 1993, the *Creep* EP was released in Japan with the same track listing as the reissue of the CD single, and this country's version of *Pablo Honey* was issued with five extra tracks, treating fans to some of the more rarely heard songs from the band's set list.

Leaving Japan, Radiohead set out for Australia, where "Creep" had already fallen off the charts. There the venues were only half-full. Again the band was reminded that there were a lot more "Creep" fans in the world than Radiohead fans. They knew they would have to labor to create a real fan base. This tour also gave the band the opportunity to test-drive new material, some of which had never before been played live. "It was great," notes Ed, "because we played these new songs live and we rediscovered what the songs were about and where our strengths [lay] and what was Radiohead and what was not" (Baily).

After Australia, the band played a couple of shows in New Zealand before returning home to hit the Glastonbury main stage. It was to be their first British festival appearance. Their Glastonbury lineup contained a few new songs, which had also been played at the Astoria show in May, including "Just," "Bones," and "Maquiladora." It was a great performance, and an illuminating experience for the band: "I've never really understood the appeal of standing in a field not being able to hear the band," remarked Thom, "but I could after [our performance]. There was such an amazing atmosphere" (Collis, "Videohead").

After Glastonbury, the band did one more show and then returned to the studio to complete the new album. This time the recording session took place at the Manor in Oxfordshire. Within two weeks, the album had pretty much come together, and Radiohead had managed to analyze what they had already put on tape. They didn't really like what they heard. As they had performed certain songs live, on tour, these compositions had grown, and band members now questioned whether some of the tracks that had been laid down beforehand truly reflected the sound they were striving for.

During the next stretch in the studio, at the Manor, they had recorded "Bones" as well as another version of "The Bends," both on the same day. Leckie disliked what they had done to "The Bends"; he

Jonny playing at The Powerhouse in London, England, 1992

thought that the guitars were too loud, that the track in general was overblown. Radiohead, however, insisted it was a great recording, and the track made it onto the album. The recording of "Bullet Proof . . . I Wish I Was" began with just the bass and drum lines. Ed and Jonny were supposed to add layers to this but didn't know what direction to take. Leckie isolated them in soundproof rooms and they created a range of noises without hearing what was on the track. Six tapes of noises later, the song came together.

Leckie took the tracks back to Abbey Road Studios after these sessions, his main priority being to mix the songs that would be on the band's 1994 double EP *My Iron Lung*: "Punchdrunk Lovesick Singalong," "Lozenge of Love," "Lewis [Mistreated]," "Permanent Daylight" (another song recorded by Radiohead with the help of Godrich), and an older recording, "You Never Wash up after Yourself." The record company had begun to ask him for multitracks of songs set for the album, sending them off to Kolderie and Slade to be mixed at Fort Apache Studios. "The annoying thing for me a little bit was that there are things on there that they'd told me not to do originally," says Leckie of the album versions — "like use big reverbs on the voice or use certain tones that were forbidden — that the Americans did. The final product is a lot harder. I don't think I could have got it sounding quite as blasting as that" (Doyle, "Diary").

While Kolderie and Slade were mixing the album, Radiohead took to the road again. Playing the Reading Festival, the band went against conventional wisdom and played almost all new material. Hufford found the performance embarrassing. He could not believe that Radiohead was refusing to feed the audience familiar material. A joke went around that day that Hufford talked only about his other band, the Oxford trio Supergrass, which had recently joined his stable.

On 23 September 1994, Radiohead returned to Abingdon to play at the Old Gaol. It was a charity gig for Rwanda. They raised 7,000 pounds for the cause. (This show wasn't the band's only attempt to aid a charitable organization: they had also donated a studio version of "Banana Co." to a compilation called *Criminal Justice! Axe the Act*, the proceeds of which went to the Coalition Against the Criminal Justice Act in Britain.) Only three days after the gig at the Old Gaol, the *My Iron Lung* double EP was released in England. The EP only made it to number 24 on the charts, which wasn't too surprising because, like the *Pablo Honey* releases, it wasn't getting the necessary exposure. Radio 1 decided the song wasn't right for their listeners — it was too raucous — so they left it off the playlist.

My Iron Lung was released all over the world in different formats. Only the Australian version contained all the B-sides that were on the British EPs; other countries got a selection of three or four B-sides. While it was released as a between-album EP in other countries as well, it was not considered a very serious effort. Perry Watts-Russell, Capitol's vice president of A and R, notes of the EP: "That was only meant to be a fanbase item. It wasn't a proper first single. We really didn't even pursue radio airplay for it" (Atwood, "Radiohead Creeps").

Radiohead toured the single — which dealt directly with the fame they'd acquired as a result of "Creep," and the health problems they'd faced — around England for a couple of weeks in October 1994, and then flew to North America for yet another *Pablo Honey* tour. This time, though, their destination wasn't the United States or Canada — it was Mexico, a country rarely toured by British bands. As they broached this new territory, pent-up emotions finally began to explode. "It just all came out," explains Thom — "all the stuff that we'd always been fighting and I think, when we started our little band, when we were kids at school, it was never really about being friends or anything. We were playing our instruments in our bedrooms and wanted to play them with someone else and it was just symbiotic. We never really thought about it" (Richardson). Band members found themselves clashing over things they had never really discussed before. There was yelling, tears, flashes of temper. The disintegration of Radiohead seemed imminent. But, once again, they managed to pull back before falling over the edge. Forced at last to vent their anger and frustration, band members came out of the experience feeling closer. Their reasons for being Radiohead had suddenly changed. And, the band was finding relief of another kind during this tour: trying out new material, they found themselves becoming more comfortable and happy with the songs they had written.

Ed sums it all up by saying, "We came to realize that the friendship was as important as trying to make good music" (Freeman). Phil believes such upsets are par for the course, given the inherent stresses of the music world: "I think if you speak to anybody in any band, at some points when things get particularly stressful, everybody toys with the idea of just stomping out and being a big drama queen about everything. But I don't think we ever seriously contemplated splitting the band" (Harding).

At the end of the Mexican tour, Jonny and Thom remained in North America to play two promotional shows in New York City. These were strictly acoustic gigs, and they mainly showcased the band's new material. Without much opportunity for a breather, the boys headed back to Abbey Road in early November, where they still had work to do on "Sulk" — the song just wasn't coming together. Originally planned as a single, the track had already been recorded and mixed, but the band thought their live versions sounded much better than what they had laid down in the studio. They wanted to give it another go.

The song had been written as a response to the killings in Hungerford back in 1987, but it was now seven years old. Thom realized the meaning of the lyrics would be lost on most people, so he made some revisions. He was especially concerned about the final lyric — "Just shoot your gun" — because he thought some might think it referred to Kurt Cobain, who had killed himself in April of 1994. That line became "You'll never change."

Around this time, Leckie came across a track the band had recorded as a demo only five months after *Pablo Honey* was released: "High and Dry." He thought the song was brilliant and was sure it would make a great single, but both the record company and the band insisted that it be reserved for the next album. After the mixing was completed, band members reconsidered the song and decided to add it to the current album in its raw demo version. They would have to relearn the tune; it had been a long time since they last played it.

Finally, near the end of November 1994, the album was completed. Radiohead was thrilled with the final product and felt confident about performing this material over and over again on the road. Looking back on the process of making the album, they realized how lucky they'd been to hook up with Leckie: he'd taught them so much about making records. "He demystified the whole process of recording," notes Jonny. "That helped us realize how to use the studio. Most studio people are reading science magazines about sound; ask them what music they like and they give you a blank look. It had always been hard for us to be musical in that environment. This time we found ourselves" (Randall, "Sounds"). Reflecting on the creative process they had just emerged from, Thom remarked, "There was a lot of analysing and overanalysing and anxiousness, but the first time I genuinely thought we'd moved on and killed 'Creep' was when I heard the test pressing of the new album. As soon as we'd done it, everything just opened up again: all the doors and windows just went poof! And life became a little bit simpler" (Yurkiw).

In England, EMI was unsure of the album, but the company did not stand in the band's way by demanding changes. In America, it was another story. The initial talk was to not release the new album in the United States at all, as it was not expected to achieve the sales of *Pablo Honey*. Radiohead was not willing to give up on such a vast market, and, ultimately, neither was the record company, so Thom and Jonny were sent off to do a few small shows to promote the new release. This type of tour — an East Coast gig one day and a West Coast one the next — involves a lot of air travel, which Thom hates. He has fluid in his ears, which makes him hypersensitive not only in the air but also during performances — this is why he wears earplugs when the band plays live. There is a history of deafness in his family, and the ear problems Thom is experiencing may one day lead to his own hearing loss. Because it makes him feel more like a politician on the hustings than a musician with music to share, Thom despises promotional touring anyway — the ear problems just make it worse. "We spend half our time on planes," he says, venting his contempt for the whole enterprise. "I was curious to work out what that smell is in an air plane. What is that smell? It's a combination of air conditioning and stale farts, which is a charming thought" (Bondi).

During this visit to the US, the aim of which was to turn fans on to the fact that Radiohead had more going for it than just a single, Thom and Jonny were often angry. They kept finding themselves disembarking from yet another plane only to be hustled off to play for people who stood before them chanting "Creep." They were jaded. What was the point of being in a band? Says Thom, "You do sometimes get the feeling that you're just one more element in the entertainment industry's desperate attempt to distract people from the fact that their lives are [messed] up" (Brown).

The new album — *The Bends* — was named after the song that had been in the band's roster the longest, but that title also had a larger meaning in terms of Radiohead's career. "The bends are what you get when you're scuba diving and you come up too fast," explains Thom; "you get too much nitrogen in your blood. You can die from it. I wonder if you implode or explode or what?" (Myers, "Creep Show"). Phil elaborates: "That's the whole thing of the title, *The Bends*. You can come up too quickly. And you suffer the consequences" (Cantin). In light of the illnesses the band members endured on the *Pablo Honey* tour and the content of certain songs on the album (like "Bones"), the album's title is brilliant. So is the cover: pursuing his interest in medical imagery, Thom went to a hospital where he took the pictures that were used for it.

As 1995 wore on, EMI prepared to release Radiohead's sophomore album. The band was ready for a new tour and a new life. This would be their renaissance. They'd break out of the one-hit-wonder strait-jacket and prove to the world that they deserved to be taken serious-ly. How could radio ignore these new songs? They were intelligent, personal, but still accessible. And press coverage would have to increase because band members had killed themselves in the studio to produce a perfect collection of songs. *The Bends* was a master-piece.

But anticipation for this album was not high. Few suspected what was in store. This lack of excitement was summed up by Ian Gittens in his review of the band's Glastonbury performance: "I'd love Radiohead to surprise me and produce a wealth of turbulent, tower-ing new songs to prove their rumoured greatness, but I'm not holding my breath" (Gittens).

TROUBLED WORDS OF A TROUBLED MIND?

7

"Britpop" was a term widely used in 1995 to describe a musical style that was generating a lot of interest. At the forefront of the movement were Blur, Pulp, and Oasis. Many new bands came out of nowhere to become overnight sensations, and sudden-success stories filled the British weekly and monthly journals. All you had to do to become a Britpop celebrity at this point was rip off a guitar riff from the likes of the Small Faces, the Kinks, or Wire, put a cute guy or girl in front of a microphone, and watch journalists and fans alike fall at your feet.

This is not to say no good acts came out of the scene — many excellent ones did. Bands like the Boo Radleys, Supergrass, and the Charlatans all made exceptional albums that sold well and won much-deserved admiration. The problem was that some of the newer acts had little or no experience within the music industry, making it very difficult for them to sustain a soaring career for long.

Menswe@r is one example. This novice act's first gig was covered in *Select* magazine, they made it onto *Top of the Pops* without even having a single, and they graced the stages of Glastonbury before they had released an album. Something about Menswe@r appealed to virtually everyone. If there were some universal, groundbreaking songs on their debut album, *Nuisance*, why was the band a laughing stock by the end of that year? Why were they so quickly forgotten after that? The answer is that they represented Britpop's main failing. The press had chosen to elevate bands that couldn't sustain such close attention, and then, a few short months later, music journalists abandoned those acts because they had run out of ideas.

In Britain, when Radiohead released the double-A-side single "Planet Telex" and "High and Dry," it was not surprising that the two-part EP entered the charts only at number 17 and then fell right off them. Radiohead didn't adhere to the dominant agenda of the time, and the music press didn't have the imagination to cover a band that didn't fit in the Britpop stereotype. And radio treated the band as it had always done: it ignored the new release. Thom says, "We've always been the people at the party who turn up too early and leave fairly quickly or just get drunk quickly. We never really feel like we're part of what's going on, which sometimes has made us feel out of place. It's made us feel really paranoid, but, well, fuck it. Why bother keeping up?" (Bondi).

But the quintet's fortunes were about to change. Despite the single's poor sales, the critics were beside themselves when the album, *The Bends*, finally fell into their hands. The release was deemed virtually flawless by the press on both sides of the Atlantic, and most major publications around the world awarded it top marks. Many critics had clearly listened carefully, and were able to articulate for their readers just what it was that made *The Bends* so good. This kind of media scrutiny was a new experience for Radiohead. *Vox* writer Craig McLean wrote, "Radiohead's strength is that they turn their downer on the world into something that's stridently uplifting" ("Reviews"), while Dave Morrison of *Select* enthused, "Radiohead have moved on, and offer 12 examples of why they're one of the UK's big league, big-rock assets."

Ever-modest Radiohead tried to sidestep the avalanche of compliments. They subverted praise with humor. Colin, after reading a *Rolling Stone* review that gave *The Bends* four stars, quipped, "It's four stars in quote marks. Does that mean they just swore at it?" (Mueller).

Still, the lyrics of *The Bends* were open to misreading, and many journalists interpreted the album as a sort of cry for help from Thom. This may seem like a wild assumption, but it makes sense in the context of the era. Eleven months before the release of *The Bends*, Kurt Cobain had shot himself, largely due to the resounding success of the band's single "Smells like Teen Spirit" and the pressures that came along with being thrust so rapidly into the public eye. And, in 1994, the Manic Street Preachers had released a very intense, disturbing album titled *The Holy Bible*. In February of 1995, his band's unstable songwriter and guitarist, Richey Edwards, disappeared. Many people were worried; suicide theories flew. While this possibility was later discounted, Edwards and Cobain became linked as tragic figures in the music world, stars who had crumbled beneath the weight of press and fan adulation. There were those who were convinced that the disturbing

75

Jonny

albums these two artists had made would adversely influence unstable and impressionable fans, prompting them to consider suicide.

So, when journalists saw titles like "Bullet Proof . . . I Wish I Was," or lyrics such as "I wanna be part of the human race," it is not surprising that they raised such concerns — Nirvana's *In Utero* and the Manics' *The Holy Bible* were still fresh in everyone's minds. They began questioning the band about it, and Thom was not amused. "It's not my fucking day-to-day," he declared. "It's not my life. These lyrics aren't self-fulfilling. *The Bends* isn't my confessional. And I don't want it used as an aid to stupidity and fuck wittery. It's not an excuse to wallow. I don't want to know about your depression — if you write to me, I will write back, angrily, telling you not to give into all that shit" (Morlin). If his words were harsh it was because throughout the *Pablo Honey* tour he had been subjected to a deluge of letters from people who thought that the guy who wrote "Creep" could solve all of their problems for them. Thom still thought and talked about the letter he'd received from that prison inmate, and he knew that being a songwriter didn't make him anyone's savior or spokesperson.

To compound the situation, an article had recently appeared in *Melody Maker* that misconstrued Thom's words, making him seem unstable and over the edge. Feeling constrained by journalists who went through his lyrics with a fine-tooth comb, Thom often found himself saying that the songs had nothing to do with his life; later, however, he would claim that every song meant something to him. To *Melody Maker*, he offered this insight: "I have a theory that all good music is uplifting, whether it be chirpy acoustic guitars and stuff about 'taking the weather with you,' or whether it sounds like Joy Division with lyrics about your dog dying in a well" (Morlin).

Elsewhere, Thom described the reaction to the new material that he anticipated from the fans: "I think the people who got what 'Creep' is really about will understand this [new] album deeply, and those who just came along for the ride will leave again. I hope. I was taking the piss — but only to a point. 'Creep' defined the genre, but it should have been a full stop. People should have moved on. I did" (Yurkiw). And, apparently, they had moved on. When *The Bends* was released in Britain on 13 March, it made an impressive debut at number six, proving there was great interest in what the band had to offer and that Radiohead's following was growing. While the album didn't hold onto that strong chart position — it was soon shunted to make room for Britpop titles — it didn't fall completely off the charts, as had the band's past releases.

Thom knew his band had put out a wonderful record, and while he didn't want to feed the media shark pool by making exaggerated, cocky statements, the normally self-effacing singer was quoted as saying, "I think we're the fucking coolest band of the 90s. I really do. Except for the hair" (Doyle, "New"). Fans could see Thom's shorter blond hair in Radiohead's first video for "High and Dry," a captivating clip shot in the middle of a desert with David Mould in the director's chair. Filmed in black and white, the video contains images of a lens trying to focus; the effect is to make the viewer feel like a voyeur witnessing an outdoor Radiohead performance. The rain falls, the quintet smiles. Thom wears a pin that proclaims, "I'm a creep."

Radiohead played a number of shows in England, including one memorable gig at the Forum in London. This performance was broadcast on FM radio, and from it the band culled the B-sides to various singles. Soon after this show, Thom and Jonny set off to North America again to undertake another small acoustic promotional tour. Although the band had achieved success in North America with *Pablo Honey*, they believed the new album would give them the opportunity to start afresh in the New World. They could be a (practically) brand-new band. "We were kind of discounting America pretty much, because they had us down as a pop act," explains Jonny. "Now we have record company big wigs ringing us up and telling us how we should be doing things, which is worse in a way" (Malins, "Scuba Do").

This new wave of corporate pressure began with the band's single "Fake Plastic Trees." Even given Radiohead's impeccable performance on *The Bends*, Capitol Records felt it could improve the single and ensure radio play by remixing the song, as they'd done with "Stop Whispering." "If there's one reason I'd give up this business, it's because people will try to fuck with your stuff to fit a formula," says Thom. "People say it won't work on the radio, but I have no fucking idea what they mean" (Stud Brothers). He continues: "Our so-called success in America was that it allowed us to do lots of things, but it also meant that somehow we owed somebody something. But I could never figure out who and I couldn't work out how much" (Doyle, "Party On").

In the end, the band's resistance to the company's manipulations paid off: Capitol backed off; "Fake Plastic Trees," the first Radiohead single released in both Canada and the United States, remained unchanged. Jake Scott's intriguing yet simple video of the song depicts band members in a grocery store sitting in carts. "It's basically just acoustic guitar and voice," explains Colin. "There isn't much playing until the last verse really. So we couldn't exactly have the band standing around like lemons with their instruments. It's much better to have them sitting in supermarket trolleys like lemons" (Thompson). "Fake Plastic Trees" was later released in England as well, but the single debuted at number 20 and didn't generate much radio attention. The live acoustic B-sides were so simple and beautiful — it's a tragedy that more people didn't get to hear them.

On 4 April, after the band had been in the United States a couple of weeks, *The Bends* was released. The album debuted at number 88 on the *Billboard* chart, but this time it headed downward. It would never climb back up. It seemed that in the United States the sophomore jinx was beginning to take effect, and as the band played its way through a string of American shows they couldn't manage to shake it.

On the same day Thom and Jonny performed on a special radio show, *The Morning becomes Eclectic*, for KCRW in Santa Monica, California. While most bands would have used this opportunity strictly to promote their new album, this duo decided to debut a new song — "Subterranean Homesick Alien." Influenced by the school essay Thom wrote back at Abingdon, the tune dealt with aliens coming to Earth. It would not be released for over two years.

Radiohead did a couple of US club gigs in April, and then took off for Sweden, Holland, and Italy. Next on the schedule was a brief interlude at home. In England, they performed on the late-night British television show *Later with Jools Holland*. As they delivered "The Bends" and "High and Dry" they were in top form. During the taping of the show, Thom was introduced to one of his musical heros — Elvis Costello. He was elated; he dreamt about the evening for the next six months. And Costello was impressed as well. He later remarked that Thom "threw himself into the performance, which is difficult on TV because the camera can make you look like a ranting puppet. I can think of some of my early performances which are like that" (Du Noyer).

Just a few weeks later, Radiohead members were approached with an irresistible offer, one that would allow them to meet a band that all five had long idolized. "Michael Stipe saw the 'Fake Plastic Trees' video on MTV late one night and bought the album as a result and invited us [to tour with REM]," Jonny told me. "We thought about it for a quarter of a second and then reluctantly agreed."

This tour wouldn't happen until later in the summer, giving Radiohead time to do their own major headlining *Bends* tour across the United States and Canada, where they returned to the same stages they had commanded during the *Pablo Honey* tour. They had prepared themselves for the worst, knowing that "Creep" could no longer ensure them an eager audience. They were now entering a phase of rebuilding a following from scratch. "We were kind of telling each before we left that it was going to be like starting again, and we kind of got quite excited about that idea," Jonny admitted to me. "By the time we got [to North America] for the start of the *Bends* tour it had been more than a year that we had been away, so we were kind of saying, 'Yeah, we are just starting again, playing the small clubs again, and it doesn't matter if no one comes.' But amazingly there were mostly sold-out shows, obviously on the strength of *The Bends*. I think a one-song hit doesn't keep people's interest very long. It's weird because there is kind of a core of fans in America who get the NME and who are interested in British bands, which is kind of bizarre, and we had a combination of that and a combination of people who knew *The Bends*, so it was cool!"

Band members were thrilled with this response, proud that they'd earned it during those long months in the studio. "It's a more accurate depiction of what Radiohead are about, because on *Pablo Honey* we relied more on the producers because we had never been in the studio before," explains Colin. "So this record is us working out how to get things sounding good together, reaching for an identity. We all have regrets about the album, things we would have done differently, but that's inevitable" (Holloway).

Throughout the tour, Jonny wore an arm brace to avoid a repetitive strain injury. His style of playing made this a real danger. His technique is also so violent, so intense, that he mutilates his fingers. "I enjoy putting the arm brace on before I play," he confides. "It's like taping up your fingers before a match. It's a ritual" (Doyle, "Party On"). Radiohead vents a lot of energy and aggression onstage — nowhere else. But their opening act for this tour did not show such restraint. David Gray decided to enact a rock-and-roll cliché by destroying a hotel room with a few members of his band. The Radiohead boys went in after Gray's crew had left the hotel and cleaned up. As Jonny points out, when bands ransack the premises it's the minimum-wage cleaner who has to cope with the mess.

Hotel-room trashing will never be a Radiohead trademark. "We're all brought up in middle class Oxford, and there's an air of politeness that's hard to escape," says Ed (Wiederhorn, "Radiohead"). Thom describes just how "rock-crazy" Radiohead really is. If they feel an uncontrollable urge to tick people off while on tour, they employ a method that's much more diabolical than destroying rooms. "Most people throw TVs out of the windows, but we go into lobbies, find the computerized piano and turn the speed controls right up. "That's much more rock 'n' roll, especially as no one ever knows how to turn it back again. I just find it very funny" (Sutherland, "Material World").

Radiohead's image was transformed during this tour. Band members no longer felt the need to embody the British stereotype that so captivated American music journalists throughout their earlier US tours. "All that stuff about drinking tea after gigs, well, it's not so true anymore," declares Thom. "The one thing you can do on tour is drink. You drink out of boredom and frustration. It makes things a fuck of a lot easier" (Stud Brothers).

Also, with Oasis's Gallagher brothers making news for their on- and offstage quarrels, the Greenwood brothers were asked about their relationship. What was it like to tour for months on end with a sibling? Were the Greenwoods anything like the Gallaghers? Jonny answered this question for me: "No, sadly not. Colin is kind of the opposite. He is into affection and he keeps hugging me and telling me that I'm his brother, as if I didn't know that. Kind of a long, drawn-out 'You're my brother.'" Colin likes to wear a badge on his coat that reads, "I have a baby brother." But Colin, when confronted with the Gallagher comparison, muddies the waters: "Unlike the Gallaghers we beat each other up in private and get on very well in public" (Morris).

While the general public perception of Radiohead was that the band was comprised of five very intelligent, levelheaded musicians, Thom's individual image was continually distorted in the media. Some days, he'd be depicted as a sort of tortured artist, other days, as a complete bastard. His bandmates began to be disturbed by this negative attention: says Colin, "People try to pin this persona on him that has nothing to do with him" (Hendrickson). Reminiscing about the Exeter days, sHack offers this insight. "Thom was enigmatic," he told me. "He never tolerated fools gladly and, as such, used to get a fair bit of bad press from people who didn't know him. They would often consider him to be cold, rude even, but he simply wasn't willing to trade off his time on people he didn't like, and Exeter was the type of university where there were plenty of those about. As you got to know him, you realized that he was deeply sincere, a little bit insecure and sometimes moody, and a fanatic when it came to both his artwork and his music. He was quite a serious person as far as students go, but wasn't opposed to getting as unhinged as anyone else. He had strong-felt political views — as we all did — and used to get involved on the frontline if it was something he believed in."

Clare Kleinedler, a contributing editor at the online magazine *Addicted to Noise*, has interviewed Radiohead a few times. She described for me her first meeting with Thom. As she approached him to begin the interview, he said, "I just got here! Leave me alone!" Unfortunately, isolated comments such as this have often become the focus of articles. Over time, Kleinedler has been able to gain a better understanding of Radiohead members, though she doesn't claim to know them well. "My first meeting with Thom was not the best," she says. "He was in a really really bad mood and snapped at me quite fiercely. But later, when I brought it up to him, he was extremely apologetic and explained why he was in such a foul mood that day. The band had just gotten off a plane and were sped off to the show (it was one of those radio-station sponsored events where ten bands were playing), and they were not allowed a sound check and the place was a madhouse. Anyone in his situation would have probably reacted the way he did, but people take more notice because he is who he is. I don't think Thom has any more bad days than the rest of us; we are just lucky because we don't have the press monitoring our every move. His bad moods are caught on record, so of course people are going to come to that conclusion about him." Thom himself confesses, "I'm always losing my temper, and it's very rarely justified. I always feel myself doing it, but I can't stop it" (Sutherland, "Material World"). Phil's explanation is that Thom "doesn't like to feel satisfied. When things are going well, he will throw things off balance so that he'll be in a state of flux. That's the way he works best" (Wiederhorn, "Radiohead").

The issue of Thom being suicidal was continually brought up during the tour. Ed tried to put this idea to rest by making such honest, heartfelt comments as, "Of course one worries about Thom in the sense that one worries about a friend when they're down, but I don't worry about him being suicidal. For whatever reason someone drives themselves to suicide, Thom is not suicidal and he doesn't want to project himself as a magnet for people with suicidal tendencies. I worry about him when he's down or on tour like I worry about Colin, Phil, or Jonny, but I don't worry about him taking his own life" (Berketo).

"We're a mess. But it's a great mess, a glorious mess," concludes Thom (Reid).

This "mess" found themselves enjoying the Beverly Hills high life that summer. A couple of the band's songs were used in the hit movie

Clueless, a smart (despite its title) comedy that poked fun at all of the Beverly Hills–based TV shows that were invading the airwaves. The film's lead character, Cher (played by Alicia Silverstone), hears an acoustic version of "Fake Plastic Trees" on her stepbrother's radio and complains about the "maudlin music of the university station." There are two other interesting Radiohead moments in the film: the first occurs right after Cher fails her driving test, when a slowed-down acoustic intro to "My Iron Lung" is heard; the second is when Cher is listing the pros and cons of her stepbrother and notes that he listens to "complaint rock." Says Colin, "There is an early modern English literary analogy to that, which is the poetry of complaint. Basically, it was an oral tradition in which the peasants bemoaned their losses. And, of course, 'complaint can also mean illness.' So it's good to see that Alicia has a good grounding in literature," (Collis, "Radiohead"). And Thom adds, "The characters in that film aren't the kind of people I'd want to like Radiohead. They're just average, two-dimensional Beverly Hills kids, and the person who is actually listening to us in the film is the only three-dimensional character" (Sutherland, "Material World").

Bands, of course, can't handpick their fans, but Radiohead often lashes out at the morons in their audiences who don't attend concerts for their love of the music but to prove that their testosterone levels are high. During their summer club tour of the United States, the band's disgust with that sector of their fan base grew. More and more moshers were pushing and shoving other concertgoers, and ruining their Radiohead experiences. "It seems the people who are into moshing are those people from college who you detested, the sports jocks," says Ed — "the ones who normally stayed away from so-called alternative shows, and who were seen at a Van Halen or Bon Jovi show, and now think alternative music is their thing. And that's fine, I'm very much for winning those people over, but don't bring your fucking bullying instincts to one of our gigs where there are young girls and blokes out there." He then jokes, "Maybe we should have a cage at stage right, like Metallica. We could throw them meat during the show" (Dawn).

These rambunctious kids who would prefer to mosh than listen to the music may have been goaded by *Beavis and Butthead*. In 1995, the two animated television junkies gave another stamp of approval to Radiohead, proclaiming that "Fake Plastic Trees" was a great song to "mellow out to" — it had even helped Beavis to work off a "boner." After mulling over who Thom reminded them of, they decided he looked like Ed Grimley, the hopeless nerd character created by comedian Martin Short of SCTV and *Saturday Night Live* fame.

Radiohead's US tour wound down in the middle of June, and the band headed over to Japan for a few shows. There, Phil met up with the members of a fanclub that had been formed in his honor — the "Phil Is Great" club. This club was created so that no member of the band would feel overlooked — often the case with drummers. "It's in Osaka," explains Phil. "It was strange playing gigs over there, going to play a show and then spot someone wearing a 'Phil is Great!' T-shirt. Only in Japan, I suppose" (Dawn).

It wasn't long before Radiohead was back in North America. This time, they would do a club tour, and their opening act would be Drugstore, good friends of theirs. They made some unconventional stops — two dates in Arizona, a show in Carrboro, North Carolina, and one in London, Ontario — in an effort to expand their fan base by hitting places that normally wouldn't get an act of Radiohead's stature.

In the weeks following this short club tour, Radiohead returned home to do a crucial series of dates that would not only teach them a lot more about the nature of the music business, but would also allow them to form an important bond with a quartet of American heros.

I FEEL MY LUCK COULD CHANGE

8

"Hi, I'm Michael. I'm really glad you could do this. I'm a very big fan" (Yorke). The Radiohead boys are unlikely to forget these words. While they had enjoyed a lot of adulation after the release of their second album, this praise was different — it came from such a musically intelligent, innovative, and talented source. Michael was Michael Stipe, lead singer of REM, and the occasion was the inauguration of the REM/Radiohead tour of Europe. Radiohead was about to learn what a band can expect when it reaches the level of stardom that REM had attained.

The Athens, Georgia–based band was on the road to support *Monster*, but the tour's success was not resting on sales of this album alone; REM had not toured its two previous, extremely successful albums, *Out of Time* and *Automatic for the People*. Awards and gold discs were bestowed upon REM in the countries they toured, and they always invited Radiohead along to the award ceremonies. Watching their mentors handling themselves in these situations, Radiohead members realized that no matter how famous they might get, some things wouldn't change. "They all pose and smile and do the whole political bit and are extremely nice," remarked Thom. "I'm shocked. It seems you have to be nice to people forever. I may as well get used to my cracked smile" (Yorke).

On 3 August, only a few days into the tour, during an informal backstage session that included members of REM, Thom introduced a new song, "No Surprises, Please." It drew a tremendous response from the small gathering, though the tune wouldn't make it into Radiohead's live set for a few more months. That session demonstrated to REM what Radiohead was capable of, and turned the American musicians, especially Stipe, into even bigger fans.

85

Radiohead clearly had a great deal to offer — now and further down the road.

The next day, Thom and Michael spent a bit of time together, but Thom's worship of Michael made things awkward. Stipe tried to relax the British singer by telling him about the first time he met his own idol, Patti Smith. This turned out to be an effective icebreaker. Their friendship grew strong over time; Stipe helped and advised Thom, who was still having problems with the touring, the "Creep" phenomenon, and the press. Just sitting and talking with such an accomplished musician — Stipe had several huge, worldwide hits under his belt — Thom began to develop a sense of how intense fame could be handled. His bandmates also came away from the tour with a new perspective on the music business. "It was breathtaking, really," Jonny told me. "We had sound check every single night and [REM] would watch us from the wings every night and would have comments about new songs and stuff. I was a bit nervous at first because I thought they would be really unenthusiastic about music and really sick of touring and really sick of writing songs and stuff, but it was the complete opposite. I also ended up kind of getting this huge musical crush on some of the ways they write and play, especially [bassist/backup vocalist/keyboardist] Mike Mills. I realized he is the hidden star, really."

Radiohead's last day of the European leg of the REM tour was spent in Tel Aviv, Israel, where "Creep" had been such a hit. Thom went out for dinner with REM members that night, and a young fan approached their table to ask for Thom's autograph — not Stipe's. Thom was extremely embarrassed, but the REM boys thought it was hilarious.

Leaving the REM tour for a few weeks (the two acts would reconvene later for a month of shows in the United States), Radiohead played festivals in Denmark, Holland, and Switzerland. Around this time, a new two-part Radiohead single was released: "Just." It made it to number 19. Many reviewers noted the similarities between the guitar lines in this song and those found in the music of Magazine. It seems that Susan Greenwood had truly influenced her little brother's musical formation, but it was not until one of the band's sound men played Magazine to Jonny that he believed there was any similarity. "It was scary how I'd been ripping off John McGeogh even though I hadn't started playing guitar until I was fourteen," he says. "Thank God my sister wasn't playing me AC/DC or something" (Doyle et al.).

The single was accompanied by one of the most talked-about videos of the year, which proved that Radiohead was taking the video-making process very seriously and creating high-quality, thought-provoking short films. Jonny explained to me, "I think we got really sick of a lot of the whining that goes on about videos by bands saying, 'Oh, I hate doing videos,' and they kind of do really bad videos as a result, or they don't do them at all. Some bands do videos really well, like REM, so I think it was just something where we decided to change our enthusiasm about it and do videos well."

The "Just" clip, directed by Jamie Thraves, was filmed over three days. As the band plays, they stare out of an apartment window; this is intercut with footage of a man lying in the middle of a sidewalk. He is unable to tell the crowd that is forming around him why he's there. After much begging, arguing, and pleading, all communicated with subtitles, the prone man gravely tells the crowd why he is on the ground. His explanation is not subtitled. We then see the entire crowd lying on the ground. We are left extremely confused. "I love the idea of no one knowing it," says Thom. "I don't understand why I haven't heard from any lipreaders yet. I just get looks of sheer frustration when I tell people I'm not going to tell them the answer" (Howell).

Band members agreed not to leak the mysterious explanation, though Jonny said in a much later interview that one lipreader had deciphered a number. He played around with me when I asked him — over the phone — about the segment. "What does he say? Oh well it's scripted, and he says that if you want to *** then you really have to ***. I think that's what he said." (The * symbols represent Jonny pushing phone buttons to mask what he was saying.) He then added, "It was all written down and scripted and decided one night after one very long session of relaxing. It's sort of as life-problem-solving as you can expect out of a late-night discussion. It sounded great at the time, but I'm not sure how helpful it would be to know it."

Thom loved the video. It captured the song exactly as he had wanted it to be. "I felt like the visuals had to stand on their own. It was always my ambition to shoot something as narrative as possible within the context of a music video. Using subtitles seemed like a natural way to achieve this, since the words do not compete with the actual vocals of the song" (Atwood). The "Just" clip was successful all over the world and was named MTV's Breakthrough Video. It also made waves on British video stations and entered the Top 30 Best Videos of All Time for 1995 on Canada's MuchMusic station.

The band's formidable musical skills improved still more in the weeks after the release of "Just." On 4 September, Radiohead entered a recording studio, where they met up with many other British acts,

EBET ROBERTS / REDFERNS

Some nights are more interesting than others

each set to record a track for a special compilation titled *Help!*, a fundraiser for the victims of the war in Bosnia. The project was the brainchild of Tony Crean, the marketing manager of Go! Discs. Along with publicists Terry Hall and Anton Brookes, Crean decided to put an album together in a very unusual fashion: a selection of bands would record songs on a Monday and the resulting album would hit the stores by Saturday of the same week. This emphasized the urgency of the cause.

The first and most popular band asked to participate was the Stone Roses. When they said yes others followed suit — including Oasis, Massive Attack, the Boo Radleys, and Suede. Jonny was the first Radiohead member interested in contributing a track, but soon all the boys were eager to delve into the project. The band had a song kicking around that they all loved — "Lucky" — and this was the perfect opportunity to record it. An exploration of happiness, it encapsulated the feelings of the fivesome at this time; the elation of the REM tour hadn't yet worn off.

"The two charity things that we've done, the *Criminal Justice* record and [*Help!*], have been things that we felt really strongly about and that had something a bit different about them," explained Ed ("Stars"). The recording date was set for 4 September, but before any music was committed to tape, the various artists involved were subjected to a few hours of interviews that were to be used for a documentary film about the album. The musicians answered questions and pretended to be in the process of recording their songs (yes, that's right, they're just lip-synching in the video footage).

Nigel Godrich, who had been studio engineer for *The Bends*, produced Radiohead's contribution. "Lucky" was an absolute success, not just in the eyes of those putting the project together, but also in Radiohead's estimation. They were hot on the idea of recording a song so quickly — especially when the final product sounded perfect. In fact, the recording went so well that the band immediately returned to the studio to lay down two more tracks, "Talk Show Host" and "Bishop's Robes," the latter dealing with Thom's hatred for his Abingdon headmaster. These tracks were recorded with the same lightning speed, and the results were astonishing. Ed even believes that the three days of studio time it took to lay down these two songs and "Lucky" constituted Radiohead's best recording session ever.

And there was another reason 1995 was a special year for Thom. He was finally able to put a big chunk of his musical earnings into something he'd been wanting for some time. A home. "Basically I want to have a house that 'Creep' built," he joked. "And I actually want to call it The House of Creep" (Bondi). So he and Rachel moved into a house that had extra bedrooms for visiting friends and a pond in the backyard. In an un-rock-and-roll fashion, he secured a 25-year mortgage at a fixed rate. Always the money-conscious musician. But, as it turned out, Thom was rarely there because the band had very little time off in 1995.

Soon after completing the *Help!* project, they took off for Miami where they reunited with REM for a month-long amphitheater tour of the United States. During this final stretch with REM, Radiohead got an even stronger sense of what massive popularity was like. "We had this chat with Michael Stipe," says Colin. "Stipe always gives a speech before they start to do ['Losing My Religion'], saying 'This isn't our song anymore. This is your song.' The fact that we were still doing 'Creep,' he thought, was pretty cool" (Considine). Thom likes to make speeches before playing "Creep," and while he admits to feeling the same way about this song as Stipe feels about "Losing My Religion," he rarely betrays it during the band's set. Instead, he routinely gives "Creep" introductions like these: "We still play this song because it's a good song"; "I don't know what this one's called"; and, "This is the one you have in karaoke machines, but it's a good song."

During this opening stint with REM, Radiohead began to test out a few new songs while doing their sound checks, though they would not become part of the concert lineup for quite some time. These were "Climbing up the Walls," "Let Down," and "An Airbag Saved My Life," which REM enjoyed. Stipe was again able to witness Radiohead's talent and innovation: during one show he said to the audience, "Radiohead are so good they scare me" (Doyle, "Party On").

The tour concluded on 1 October, in Hartford, Connecticut. Since REM is notorious for their bizarre farewells to support acts, and since before taking the stage Radiohead members were warned not to wear clothes they ever wanted to wear again, the British musicians were a bit anxious about what would happen at the end of their set. Throughout the show, Stipe played with a remote-control car, running it around the stage, often by Ed's feet. At the end of their set, Radiohead tossed aside their instruments and ran offstage. Then REM emerged nonchalantly from the other side of the stage equipped with glasses and a bottle of champagne, intent only on offering thanks to their new friends. Radiohead's clothes and dignity were spared on this very memorable night.

A few days after leaving REM to join the Soul Asylum tour, Radiohead's luck ran out. In Denver, on the first night of this tour, Radiohead's gear was stolen from their hotel. Still, the incident didn't devastate them as it might have other bands. "I don't think we are actually that attached to our gear in that sort of guitar-magazine level of attachment to one's guitars and stuff," Jonny said to me. "It was kind of annoying rather than kind of gut-wrenching. We didn't exactly have anything old or valuable. We just had things that we'd had for a long time. It was a bummer in that sense, but it wasn't kind of, 'Oh man, my '62 Sunburst' it was more kind of, 'Oh no, my 1987 guitar I bought with my grant money when I was a student.'" When I asked about the worst day of 1995, Jonny cracks, "Going to Denver and having our gear stolen on the Soul Asylum tour of all places. Kind of a triple bummer." The up side to the robbery was that the band had to cancel a few shows and go to Los Angeles to buy new equipment. The day those purchases were made was 7 October, Thom's birthday.

Back on the road, Radiohead debuted another new song, "Man-o-War." They played it only a few times in 1995, and never again after that, but many fans expect it to show up on a future release.

On 16 October, the *Help!* EP was released. "Lucky" was chosen to be the lead-off single. While this was very exciting for the band, the Radio 1 people didn't concern themselves with the quality of the song that was sent to them — they felt they had done enough for various charity releases, and opted not to play this one. Due to the lack of airplay (by now a Radiohead tradition), the single debuted at number 51 on the singles chart before falling off. "[It] was kind of embarrassing for us, because we sort of felt that we'd [contributed] this duff song," Jonny said to me, but the *Help!* organizers "were fine about it because it ended up going on a compilation record and they got loads of money for that." It "says a lot about the British radio system." Thom joked, "We're waiting for the karma police to come and sort it out" (Collis, "Radiohead").

As the end of the Soul Asylum tour approached, Thom's health once again became a problem. This time it was his vocal cords. When these things happen in the entertainment industry, the promoters step in. They have a large amount of money at stake in the shows they put on, and cancellation is not an attractive option. Many call in doctors to offer quick and simple solutions. Thom began to notice a pattern: he was prescribed drugs that helped in the short term but did nothing for him in the long run.

Radiohead completed the United States leg of their tour and

returned to England to play a series of gigs. Sparklehorse, a relatively new American band, opened for them. Members of the two bands immediately hit it off. The Radiohead boys were astounded at how talented Sparklehorse was. After Sparklehorse left the tour, Radiohead hit Spain, France, and Italy with former road companions Drugstore as their opening act. And while the tour seemed to be going well, Thom's health was deteriorating. The physicians he consulted, concerned primarily with short-term results, were giving him bad advice. On 25 November, in Munich, Germany, a doctor told Thom to take steroids to ward off laryngitis. Thom, sick and fed up, refused. He walked onto the stage that night, performed five songs, blacked out, and collapsed. Coming to, he immediately hauled himself onto his feet and left the stage, knowing he wouldn't be able to continue. At that point, he had been on the road for ten straight months with very little down time. Some unsympathetic audience members expressed their disapproval, and *New Musical Express* later reported that Thom had thrown a fit and abandoned the show.

Back on the road, Thom struggled on, knowing that the tour's end was only a few weeks away. On 3 December, between a show in Sweden the night before and a show in Amsterdam, Radiohead members found themselves in London at the *Smash Hits* poll-winners party. The event was staged by the teen mag *Smash Hits*, normally a promoter of mainstream pop — boy and girl dance acts like Take That or Louise. Such acts were on hand that night, but the bill was expanded to include a few guitar acts — at this year's party Radiohead was to perform "My Iron Lung."

Sandwiched in among such mainstream pop acts as East 17 and Take That, whose dance moves and tight abs were as important to fans as their funky beat, it's not surprising that Radiohead didn't fare well. "We stood at the side of the stage for half an hour before we went on and it was bedlam — all these girls just screaming and screaming," recalls Ed. "And then we went on, there was this awkward silence and then the screaming started again — for entirely different reasons. It seemed like the entire audience suddenly burst into tears . . . and demanded to be taken to the toilet" (Sutherland, "Rounding the Bends"). As the band left the stage, Take That singer Mark Owen pulled Ed aside and told the guitarist that he was a huge fan of Radiohead. Support often comes from the most unexpected sources.

Back on the road, Radiohead made a stop in Brussels, on the night of 5 December. It was the final show of the band's tour with their pals

Drugstore, and to mark the occasion singer Isabella Monteiro performed a special song — called "My Radiohead" — which contained the chorus, "They'll leave you high and dry / They'll take you to the bends / I feel lucky tonight / With a fake plastic tree / In my hand / It's time to say goodbye."

Radiohead also debuted their own special song on this evening, one that they would never play again. Titled "True Love Waits," it's the kind of tune that every fan falls in love with instantly (the show was bootlegged, so the song, inaccessible to the record-buying public, is familiar to tapers). The performance was acoustic, and the song's lyrics and music were breathtakingly beautiful. It seemed clear to most fans in attendance that evening that they were being treated to a taste of the band's third album.

In the final weeks of 1995, *The Bends* was honored on year-end charts all over the world. *Mojo* called it the best album of the year, *Select* placed it in the top five, even *People* magazine called it one of the great albums of 1995. The band's name cropped up in almost every music publication. They were credited with making an outstanding contribution to the world of music. At last, the British press was won over. In the UK, music journalists had kind words for the band and the album, even though Radiohead had not been a part of the Britpop scene, which had obsessed most of those scribes throughout the year. "There are two styles of bands that do well in England," Jonny explained to me. "Bands like Blur and Oasis who do get written about a hell of a lot as well as having large numbers of people going to their concerts, and bands like us and people like Massive Attack and Portishead who we get on with a lot better than some of these guitar bands. Whenever they review a concert or an album they write a lot about them, but they will never write about them from week to week, and they won't go looking for stories like they will with other bands. Whenever these bands do anything it is treated with seriousness and respect, and I would rather be in that position than be in the gossip page every week." Notes Thom: "Buy the *Guardian* and there's Jarvis Cocker [of Pulp] telling his life story again. I find this obsession with personalities offensive. I find it offensive that I have to read about Noel and Liam's extremely banal antics" (Collis, "Radiohead").

All this celebration of Radiohead caught the attention of Tony Wadsworth, managing director of the band's record company. He knew that Radiohead would have a difficult time fighting off the competition in the race of the Christmas singles, but he also realized that the band's name would be fresh in the minds of British music buyers for weeks after the festive season, due to all the accolades *The Bends* was reaping in the year-end reviews. So Wadsworth decided to wait until after the holiday season to launch the Radiohead offensive. On 22 January, "Street Spirit (Fade Out)" was released as a new single. The move was pure genius. The double EP shot onto the charts, landing at number five, even though the by-now-predictable Radio 1 wouldn't play it (because it was too somber). *The Bends* hit number four on the album charts the same week. Suddenly Radiohead was again a hit, this time in the elusive British market.

While Radiohead was busy making headlines, so was Jonathan Glazer, who had directed a stunning video for "Street Spirit" utilizing special camera techniques to make the images move at different speeds. "In this video, we wanted to make something really elegant and beautiful," declares Thom. "The song, 'Street Spirit,' came out of a stream of consciousness, and Jonathan Glazer and I wanted something that would create space in the viewers' imagination to complement this. Pop videos can so often kill a song stone dead, but when Jonathan suggested using the photosonics ultra-slow-motion camera coupled with reference to the surrealist photographers of the early century, we knew we had something" ("Videohead").

Unlike on previous occasions when singles were released, the Radiohead boys were now too busy to tour England. They were preparing to record again. This time, however, they wanted to avoid the studio experience. "I just don't think that we've ever worked particularly well in studios," Phil admitted to me. Colin interjected, "It's like you walk into a studio wearing your jacket, and it's like someone takes it off and puts [on] the studio's jacket and you're wearing someone else's clothes and feeling like you're in someone else's space. And this set of clothes has been worn by hundreds of other people."

And so Radiohead went the unconventional route. They had an old apple shed converted into a studio in a secret location outside of Oxford and called their makeshift facility Canned Applause. The record company had issued these instructions: "Take as long as you want, record it wherever you want, with whomever you want" (EMI). This time, Radiohead did as they were told.

NOBODY TELLS YOU WHAT TO DO, BABY

9

Throughout January, the first month in the studio, Radiohead practiced. They improved on their songs as they played around with them. Having bought over $140,000 worth of gear, it was also time to experiment with their new toys, to figure out how these gadgets could be used to transform the music they were about to record. Joining them in the studio again was John Leckie's engineer, Nigel Godrich, the man who had helped Radiohead record "Lucky," "Talk Show Host," and "Bishop's Robes." Since band members thought these songs ranked among their finest recordings, they were convinced that with Godrich on board this studio experience would be their best ever. Besides, Godrich had actually built Canned Applause and helped pick out the gear they had bought. "They hadn't really enjoyed recording previously, so they figured if we could make an environment where everybody feels comfortable, it would be a real bonus," Godrich explains ("Making of OK Computer").

But while Godrich was a crucial element in the creation of OK Computer, Radiohead never relinquished creative control. Band members strongly believed that there was no point in hiring a producer if that person couldn't import something to the music that they could not. So they produced the record themselves. As studio engineer, Godrich (who was the same age as the Radiohead boys) wouldn't impose any creative constraints or take the music in a direction the band didn't want it to go. "Nigel is a very positive and emotionally engaging person," says Thom, "and that's what we needed. We needed someone who was passionate and shared our taste in music" ("Making of OK Computer").

While making their album in secrecy, the band didn't stay out of the public eye. In February, Radiohead lent its support to Rock the Vote, a campaign in which bands help motivate young British voters to cast their ballots. The members of REM had participated in a similar campaign in the United States, and Radiohead had noted that it was possible to bring the message home without shoving it down fans' throats. The Rock the Vote initiative led to the release of a compilation CD, titled *Rock the Vote*, to which Radiohead contributed the Hexadecimal Remix of "Planet Telex."

The cause, Ed stated, was one he really believed in. "One of the reasons it struck a chord with me is that I have to admit that at the last General Election I didn't vote, because I was disenchanted with politics. The figures Rock The Vote sent us estimated that in 1992, 43% of those under the age of 25 who were eligible to vote didn't vote. That's 2.5 million people. Those kind of statistics are quite frightening. It means that we could have had a different government in power for the last four years" ("Vote"). Informed about political issues and able to make reasonably educated comments about the current state of the nation, Radiohead members were a boon to the Rock the Vote movement.

In the studio, the band was working out songs that had been written on the road over the past year — the same process they'd used when making *The Bends*. Thom would come up with a theme or even just a good title, and from there he and Jonny would go on to hone the general idea until they had something. "I don't think I've got any special talent," Jonny admitted during our conversation. "Thom's weird, and sometimes he lacks confidence about music, and I come at songwriting from a completely different angle, which he enjoys, I think. He doesn't like to learn too much. He admires people like Elvis Costello whose knowledge is fairly limited but who write amazing songs, but I sort of want to learn about music without buying *Guitar Player* and working out those wingy solos. I think about music in a different way from him, so he likes doing stuff with me because I kind of will do the opposite of what he is doing, and I think that can be helpful."

Enhancing and developing their songs further, taking them to a higher level, the band entered a wildly unpredictable phase of creation. "The most exciting time for me is when we've got what we suspect to be an amazing song, but nobody knows what they're gonna play on it," notes Jonny. "And that's the best feeling. Because that's when something happens. You should watch us rehearse. Everyone just clusters around their own individual amp, working stuff out. All you can hear is drums and Thom's vocals. And after a week or a day — or an hour — people tentatively turn up and say, 'What do you

London School of Economics, 1988

London School of Economics, 1988

Jonny taking a photo of a journalist

TIMOTHY NUNN/S.I.N.

Thom at Glastonbury, 1997

PREMIER

think?' It's the best part of being in a band in a way. That, and the gigs" (Bailie, "Viva la Megabytes").

With four years of touring behind them, the members of Radiohead were much better musicians than they were when they worked on *Pablo Honey*. Colin had taken bass-guitar lessons during breaks in the *Bends* tour, improving the technical aspects of his playing. The basslines he developed for the new material were more challenging than ever before. Jonny had embarked on a relentless quest for a new and unusual chord to play using both the Internet and the band's newsletter, *W.A.S.T.E.*, along the way. He wanted to know whether any guitarists among Radiohead's fans could come up with such a chord. Unfortunately, the best he got was a G minor seventh and diminished B, which he already knew, so he took solace in tinkering with his new toys. Expressed through these instruments, certain songs began to take on new life. A song like "Subterranean Homesick Alien," which, until it was recorded, had been played live as a guitar-oriented number, was transformed when electric piano was added. By March, the band had worked out arrangements for most of the *OK Computer* songs. Jonny realized that he hadn't been using his guitar much — more and more, he found himself sitting at a Hammond organ.

Overall, in the studio Radiohead can be classified as an experimental band. Describing their unusual approach, Jonny says: "We don't ruminate over which combination of amplifier, cabinet or guitar is going to make the best sounds. You lose interest if you worry about sounds or tones so much. We just work blind, in a kind of panic. It's all done in a bit of a fury, really" (Vaziri).

When "High and Dry" was released in North America as a CD single, Radiohead crossed the pond once more. A new Radiohead video had also just hit music stations. The band had been unhappy with the original clip for the song, shot in a desert setting, so Paul Cunningham was recruited to direct another one. This short film was to be Cunningham's debut. The narrative concerns two young people who have just pulled off a robbery. Making their way to a small diner where they have arranged to collect their money from the man who hired them, they are instead given a bomb. A mysterious man with a briefcase is somehow involved with the bomb, as is a chef who plants the device in the robbers' doggy bag. Radiohead plays a small role in the video, but there are no performance sequences.

The song caught on so strongly in the United States that the band was asked to play it on *The Tonight Show* on 15 March. After this, the band toured the United States and Canada, playing a set composed mainly of songs from *The Bends*, though they also added a few new numbers. One, "I Promise," was greatly influenced by REM. The two others they seemed to play almost every night were "Electioneering" and "Lift." The latter caught the interest of the audience and most of the journalists who reviewed the tour shows. It seemed almost certain that Radiohead had a winner on its hands, a vehicle that would carry them even higher.

Capitol's US reps were convinced that the catchy, rock-oriented "Electioneering" could be sold to American audiences. Radiohead's third album, they reasoned, would need the momentum of a powerful single. *The Bends* still hadn't outsold *Pablo Honey* in the US, though it had surpassed the debut in every other country.

That Radiohead had conquered Canada was most evident in Toronto, where the band played to a sold-out arena: over 4,500 people, all diehard fans, sang along to most of their songs. Amid the kind of screaming and cheering more often heard in larger venues, Jonny told the crowd that he could feel the love in the air. It was now clear that the hunger for new material was growing acute among Radiohead fans. Gone were the days when "Creep" was the only thing they wanted on the menu. "It's a weird kind of pressure," Jonny said to me. "It's pressure from people who write to us who like the music, which is weird, rather than pressure from record companies and stuff like that. But that's kind of a nice pressure, it's like something is expected from us. It's a really nice feeling in a way. You could really let it get to you, but in a way it sort of makes you feel like it's worth doing what you can to make it sound good, if that doesn't sound too cheesy." And Colin explained to me, "We've always had pressure ever since we started, and I don't think it was a dissimilar experience this time. We've been going now for nearly eleven years, since we started at school, and ever since we first started we've always put pressure on ourselves to actually improve on what we've done, to push our arrangements and push our level of performance."

A few days after the Toronto performance, Thom found himself on a radio show in Rockville, Maryland, where he played a five-song acoustic set. Here he introduced a new composition, "Motion Picture Soundtrack." The song was moving and lyrically complex, the performance stunning. In fact, all the songs the band was previewing were strong and intriguing, fueling the expectation that Radiohead's third album would be an absolute masterpiece.

Back in Europe, Radiohead played two dates in France and a couple of festivals, including the Pinkpop Festival in Holland where they were headliners. Ignoring the rain, Radiohead delivered an excellent set during which they unveiled still more new songs. Also around this time, *Mojo* magazine honored Jonny by inscribing him on its critics'-pick list of the all-time hundred greatest guitarists. Jonny was number 96, exceptional for a young, contemporary player. And he was one spot above John Squire of the Stone Roses, a guitarist many music fans believe can do no wrong. *Mojo* noted that Jonny's musical high point was his tremolo solo on "Just" (Doyle et al.).

After the Pinkpop Festival Radiohead returned to Canned Applause. Over the course of the next four weeks, the quintet cut loose. They had a great time in their personal, secluded studio, playing new songs and pushing boundaries. When they could play no more, band members went back to their Oxford homes to rest or headed for the pubs, where they hung out with friends.

"We had a lot of fun in the fruit farm when we recorded there," Ed said to me when we talked about Canned Applause. "I mean, there was no pressure in that four weeks, and we thought there was something strange about that, because this was basically our rehearsal room outside of Oxford, so we go home at eleven each night after spending the whole day recording. And there wasn't any pressure, and it was a load of fun but it was very strange. I remember thinking, 'Well, are we actually getting anything done?' And we actually did, we got a lot done." On the first day of the session, they recorded the song that Thom had debuted on the European REM tour, now titled "No Surprises." They had overworked the song, taping sixteen different versions, but it was the first take that eventually made it onto the album. "Electioneering," "Subterranean Homesick Alien," and "The Tourist" were laid down on subsequent days. "The Tourist" was the first song that Jonny had written entirely by himself.

The Tourhout and Werchter Festivals in Belgium and T-in-the-Park in Glasgow, Scotland, were next on Radiohead's agenda. At the Glasgow event, the band headlined one of the days, following Prodigy and Alanis Morissette to the stage. Then it was off to Ireland to play Dublin Olympia and another festival, Big Day Out, at the end of July. Much as the quintet might have wanted to retreat to Canned Applause after these outings, they knew that they had to continue to develop the new material in a live setting before recording it. With this in mind, they agreed to open for part of Alanis Morissette's upcoming tour of the United States. It was a pairing that Radiohead's followers could not understand. Colin attempts to explain the band's motivation: "it was silly money and it gave us a chance to work out everything live.

That, and the strangely perverse kick [we'd get] out of being these five guys in black, scaring pre-pubescent American girls with our own brand of Dark Music" (Moran). Of the Canadian chanteuse herself, Ed remarks, "Her music's pretty terrible but she's a lovely person" (Sutherland, "Rounding the Bends"). Morissette was actually a big Radiohead fan, and had been performing "Fake Plastic Trees" during all her tour gigs until the band joined her and she left the song in their capable hands.

During this tour, Radiohead hatched many new numbers, including "Climbing up the Walls," "Let Down," "Karma Police," and an extremely long composition titled "Paranoid Android." Clocking in at almost eleven minutes, it ended with a solo by Jonny on a Brian Auger Hammond. Also while crisscrossing the US with Morissette, Radiohead was approached by the producers of the movie *William Shakespeare's Romeo and Juliet* (the contemporary version, starring Leonardo DiCaprio and Clare Danes), who asked if they could use "Talk Show Host" in the film. They then sent the band a segment of the movie with the request that Radiohead do a song to accompany the credits. The quintet agreed to it all, and began work on the project when they returned to England for their next recording session.

This brief tour allowed Radiohead to overcome the mental blocks that tend to accumulate in the studio. Refreshed and well rehearsed, they were prepared to record again, but this time they didn't return to Canned Applause. Godrich and the band had decided that this phase of recording would be more fruitful if the five musicians isolated themselves from their friends and families. It was time to eliminate all distractions. They also thought it would be cool to record in a more luxurious environment — their initial idea was to find a place in France. Then Colin and Thom heard about a vacant Elizabethan mansion in Bath owned by the English star of the American TV series *Doctor Quinn: Medicine Woman*, Jane Seymour. Says Jonny: "Studios are generally very horrible places for recording — they're pretty unmusical — so we just decided to turn a big empty house into a studio, and that one was available" (Courtney).

"The first week we were there we didn't leave the house at all and after a while, it started feeling like we were on this little island separate from the rest of the universe," comments Thom. "I'd go for walks around the gardens, listening to all this music pouring out of the house in the dark, and in the background you'd hear horny vixens yowling, which is scary as hell. And I started to feel a bit . . . uneasy" (Moran). As they had while sharing that house back in 1991, the bandmates began to notice abnormal occurrences. A coterie of "horny vix-ens" inhabited the Bath mansion, and these etheral beings gradually let it be known that intruders were unwelcome. Freaked out, the band persevered, refusing to be evicted by spirits.

Before going into the studio, Thom had written the song for the *Romeo and Juliet* credits, appropriately titled "Exit Music (For a Film)." As usual, he played his brand-new composition on an acoustic guitar for the others, expecting them to suggest ways of filling out the sound. But they were at first hesitant to mess with the number. Jonny says that "Presented with a song like 'Exit Music,' which Thom just sits down and plays to you, it's impossible to know what to add to it without making it worse" (Harris, "Renaissance Men"). Finally, though, a new instrument triggered some fresh ideas, and the band focused in on "Exit Music." The day they recorded it, recalls Thom, "we received delivery of a mellotron we had bought. You can buy these remodelled, remade mellotrons that are exactly the same as the originals. So we got this thing and the first thing we did with it was all the voices on Exit Music, and after that the song came togeth-er in two days. That was the first thing that really got me, where I said 'Wow'" (Hughes).

Another song that came together in the early part of the first ses-sion was "Let Down," which the band recorded in the mansion's ball-room at three o'clock in the morning. When they had played it live on the Alanis Morissette tour, Thom opened it by playing acoustic guitar; in the recorded version, however, Jonny opens in 5/4 time while the rest of the band comes in on 4/4 time. They would later find this structure very difficult to re-create live (Randall, "Radiohead").

Many of Radiohead's new songs presented challenges. One such tune was "Paranoid Android," which had originally been three differ-ent songs that the band didn't know what to do with. Pulling them together to form one long composition that they could record, the bandmates agreed that the Hammond ending had to go, and so the song was shortened from eleven minutes to six and a half. "['Paranoid Android'] was one of the first things we finished in the sessions and we'd listen to it and we'd giggle and we felt like irre-sponsible schoolboys who were doing this thing that was just a bit of fun," says Colin. "There is a lot of humour in it, a lot of twisted humour. We'd always giggle at the end of it because we felt we'd just done this naughty thing, because nobody does like a six and a half minute song with a lot of changes" ("Radiohead Interview").

The mansion offered things a normal recording studio couldn't. For instance, the band could select a room to record in based on its unique acoustics. Phil did his drumming in a child's bedroom, and the library produced some interesting effects. The vocals for "Exit Music" were done in the front hall of the mansion. "After a few days, I think it was the fourth, actually, we began to really feel like we had a licence this time around," explains Thom. "We were getting back to that spontaneous, four track mentality that we had in the beginning. It was funny, we'd say to Nigel [Godrich], 'Can we go record in the garden?' and he'd say, 'No!,' and then I would say 'Can I do vocals in the chimney?' and he would look at me and say 'No.' He was really like a vague parental figure steering us in the right direction" (Hill).

Acoustics weren't the only area of experimentation on the new album. Radiohead started trying to imitate recordings by their favorite artists. While they admit they failed almost every time, they still manufactured some wonderful songs in the process. One person whose influence crept into a few of the new songs is Mo' Wax artist DJ Shadow, whose sample-based music crosses many genres, combining jazz, hip hop, funk, and rock. For instance, Phil sat down behind his drum kit and in fifteen minutes laid down the percussion track for "An Airbag Saved My Life," later deflated to "Airbag." Then, with a Mac and an Akai S 3000, the band cut up and altered his work, using only the best three seconds. "We took inspiration from the way DJ Shadow cut up and reassembled rhythm tracks," explains Phil. Taking those three seconds of drumming, they "put it back together to form this angular track that you don't generally get from programming or loops" (Randall, "Radiohead").

"Climbing up the Walls" also took on greater complexity, starting with the opening portion, where Colin uses a Novation Bass Station synthesizer. Claiming that he'd never seen a keyboard before, he had his brother show him what notes to play. Then they carefully prepared the instrument for live performances — Jonny put colored dots on the keys so Colin would hit the right notes. The closing chord of the song features 16 violins all playing quarter tones apart from one another. "It's the most frightening sound — like insects or something," says Jonny. "But it's beautiful" (Bailie, "Viva la Megabytes"). Of course, this assessment comes from a man who has proclaimed that he is searching for the ultimate atonal riff on all his instruments.

Varied instrumentation aside, Thom was intent on making his voice come across in a different way on every track. He worried that his brand of vocals would limit his ability to cover a range of material. "Thom said about this album anyway, he said of the 12 songs he wanted it to be sung with 12 different types of voice," explains Ed. "I think Thom at times has had a hang-up with his voice. And the fucker can sing anything — he can reduce you to tears" (Bailie, "Viva la Megabytes"). But Thom seemed to see this as the problem. As he explains, "The one reservation I had after *The Bends* was that it didn't matter what I was singing — 'Fish and chips or whatever' — it still sounded melancholic. It was frustrating, I didn't feel I could write certain songs because they didn't fit with this voice — the one I'd ended up with. So I spent a lot of time on *OK Computer* trying not to do voices like mine. The voices on 'Karma Police,' on 'Paranoid Android' and on 'Climbing up the Walls' are all different personas, though actually it's not blatantly obvious. But it was something I was acutely aware of" (Irvin).

The lyrical content of the new album also differed from that of *The Bends*, perhaps as a result of the criticism leveled at Thom after the release of that album. With one or two exceptions — "Exit Music" was a very personal song for Thom — the songs on the new album were not exercises in introspection but explorations of what was going on around him. "On this album the outside world became all there was and the most irrelevant material took on a stunning beauty and breathlessness," says Thom. "This is because I had sorted the internal stuff out. I wrote down what was around always and my singing 'identity' felt very loose. I am an airhead on this record," he adds, underplaying the complexity of the songs (Sutherland, "Rounding the Bends"). Phil expands on Thom's developing approach to songwriting: "It's got quite acerbic lyrics on top, with a different feeling underneath. It's one of our many contradictions. Even with the same song, you'll often find quite opposite feelings" (Baimbridge).

As October approached, the band took a month-long break from Jane Seymour's house. They had virtually completed recording the album, but — in typical Radiohead fashion — they found themselves analyzing the songs, rerecording certain parts, feeling insecure about accepting the first, live-off-the-floor takes of some songs as finished products. They hoped that a bit of distance would allow them a better perspective on what they had created.

During breaks from recording, their free time would fill up with tour gigs, rehearsals, and practice sessions. At one point, Thom also took the time to help Drugstore record a new song, "El President," to which he contributed some vocals. Of Radiohead, Drugstore singer Isabel Monteiro says, "They work from a very emotional level, a very intense place. When I was done [writing] that song, I thought of Thom, because he has this fantastic voice, and I wanted him to be the voice of the president" (Kaufman).

The song was recorded at Eastcote Studios. Things didn't proceed smoothly, however — the first take was a failure. Comments Monteiro: "Everyone around Thom, apart from his band, just licks his arse constantly. I think he enjoyed working with us because we don't do that. He came into the studio to do the track and the first take was terrible. It was in the wrong key for his voice and it sounded so low and mumbly! When we played it back, there's all these people sitting around the studio looking embarrassed, wondering how the hell we were gonna salvage it. So I just phoned him up, told him it was shit, and he agreed!" Thom returned to Eastcote, and, continues Monteiro, "we tweaked it up a few octaves and it came out wonderfully. He's a great person to work with, because he really appreciates honesty, and will really stick his neck out if it's something he believes in. There's plenty of shitheads in bands who aren't getting anywhere who are so far up their own arse and convinced the world revolves around them. He's in this huge band and he's still really committed to helping out others and doing his best" (Kulkarni). Due to problems with Drugstore's record label, Go! Discs, which would shortly be closed down by mother company Polygram, "El President" was not released until the spring of 1998.

During their time off in October, the Radiohead boys also worked to improve their official Web site. Since the beginning of the record-ing sessions for the new album, band members had been surfing the Internet, examining all the unofficial Radiohead sites. To their amaze-ment, they found that industrious site owners were already posting track listings, lyrics, and chord changes for the new album. It was truly astonishing: some of the songs hadn't even been recorded yet. The information was being drawn from 1995 and 1996 bootlegs. Says Ed: "One day, I'm convinced we're going to be on the Internet and we'll find an option to download an album we haven't even started recording yet. Radiohead fans are very thorough" (Moran).

Reflecting on the band's official Web site, Thom announced: "It's not gonna have much info' cos there seems to be plenty of unofficial sites who seem to know better what's going on than we do. They cer-tainly seem to be writing my lyrics for me, if I'm ever stuck for an idea I go and read them" ("Yorke Turns Net Head"). The Radiohead Web site was designed and constructed by Stanley Donwood, who had been doing the artwork for the band's covers since the *My Iron Lung* EP. Donwood worked closely with the band on the site, inviting the musicians to witness the design process and offer creative suggestions. Radiohead loved the finished product, and the site was launched at the end of October.

On the first of November, when the band was ready to go back into the studio, *William Shakespeare's Romeo and Juliet* hit movie screens across North America. The success of the film spawned an enormous demand for the accompanying soundtrack. One of the best-selling soundtracks ever released, it features a remixed version of Radiohead's "Talk Show Host." The song was used to enhance a crucial scene in the film: Romeo's parents are out looking for him; he appears onscreen, he looks up, and we hear Thom sing, "You want me." The opening guitar line from the song also appears elsewhere in the movie. "Exit Music" wasn't included on the soundtrack CD, so many Radiohead fans took their tape recorders into the theaters to make bootleg copies. Although the song was expected to appear on a later version of the soundtrack CD, Radiohead decided to pull it. "I think we knew as soon as we'd finished that it had to go on our record, and not the soundtrack," explains Jonny. "It was about more than the film, which is a bit arrogant to say, 'It's bigger than Shakespeare'" (Adams).

When the band returned to the mysterious Seymour mansion to wrap up their album, Thom again sensed that he and his bandmates were imposing their presence and music on whatever it was that lurked in there. This made him extremely uneasy; he was also very tired because he found it impossible to sleep in that charged atmosphere. "The house was . . . oppressive," he insists. "To begin with, it was curious about us. Then it got bored with us. And it started making things difficult like turning the studio tape machines on and off, rewinding them" (Blashill). Inexplicably, equipment would fail, and, after being serviced, quickly break down again. Soon band members were anxious to wrap up their recording project and get the hell out of that house. It's strange that the album's eerie tone had been planned out before the band even began recording — it was merely enhanced by the spirits that inhabited the Bath abode.

One track on the album, "Fitter Happier," embodies that enhanced eerieness. Thom got very drunk one night and made for the studio's DAT machine armed with a list he had been compiling over the previous few months — newspaper headlines he'd come across, quotations from books that had struck him as interesting. He had initially presented the list to his bandmates as lyrics for a song, but no one had been able to help him refine his jottings. Now, entering the list into the computer, playing it on a Macintosh Simpletext reader, and adding some piano accompaniment, he realized he had something. The band loved it. Thom had created a musical foundation that suited the words perfectly, thereby composing a song that would enrich the aura of the album.

By Christmas, Radiohead was finally satisfied with the recording. They had done enough, and it was time to mix. Still, things did not get any easier or move any faster. "Our problem in the studio is that we often over-analyse," remarks Ed (Kessler). During the mixing stage, the band also began considering their contribution to the *Help!* album, "Lucky." They were convinced that the song hadn't received the attention it deserved and resolved to remix the cut and put it on the album. After playing around with it for awhile, they realized it had been best in its original form and left it that way for the album.

Rumors began to circulate among Radiohead fans that the new release was going to be a double album, but the band had only briefly considered this option in the studio. They had 14 finished songs, and two were left off the album: "A Reminder" and "Polyethylene." For most bands and/or producers, such decisions can only be made near the end of the mixing and sequencing process; that is when the issue of which songs sound best together and what the overall order should be comes into perspective. "It was a pretty difficult two or three weeks where we had to argue about what went on or not," says Thom. "Because there were five of us in the band it ended up that I was having the casting vote on things, which made it hard" (Douridas). "I was going to sleep at two [in the morning] and getting up at five, because I'd have a sequence in my head," he recalls. "I'd programme it into my MiniDisc and make tapes for everybody, and send them out, and they'd go 'Thanks very much, Thom!' And then another one — 'Thanks very much, Thom!' And they didn't listen to any of them, 'cos they knew that I'd fucking lost it" (Harris, "Renaissance Men"). Various songs were considered for the opening track — "Paranoid Android," even "Fitter Happier" — but the band worried the latter choice might scare listeners off. Instead, they chose "Airbag," which provided the listener with the same type of hair-raising, eye-opening experience that "Planet Telex" had on *The Bends*.

Radiohead Web site designer Stanley Donwood also worked on the album cover, laying out the images that Thom had created specially for that purpose. While the cover was intriguing and attention-grabbing, Thom wasn't happy with the final product. "It's pretty dreadful but it's the best we could come up with at the time," he says. "But it's awful, I hate it, it's fucking rubbish." Phil completely disagreed: "Actually I love the cover, because it all came together in the same studio, and seeing it develop alongside the music, it becomes much more personal. It does have a very distinctive style, I don't think there's been a cover like that before" (Dalton).

On the inside of the cover, at the bottom of the credits page, a very Radiohead-ish remark has been inserted: "we hope that you are ok. thankyou for listening." "It was the very last thing I did and I was really, really, really drunk," recalls Thom. "I'd done all the artwork and we were just sitting there having a laugh. I typed that and it looked excellent . . . It was what you write when you've rung up someone who you haven't seen for awhile" (Dalton).

By February, the only thing the album lacked was a title. After a great deal of brainstorming, the band came up with *OK Computer*. Although this title evokes the idea of computerized sounds, slotting the album into the music world's electronica movement, the project was not, in fact, technology-oriented. Still, the title *OK Computer* held great meaning for the band. "It refers to embracing the future, it refers to being terrified of the future, of our future, of everybody else's," explains Thom. "It's to do with standing in a room where all these appliances are going off and all these machines and computers and so on, they are all going off and the sound it makes" (interview, *Studio Brussel*).

And so, over a year after the band had first entered Canned Applause, after months in a secluded studio and a poltergeist-infested mansion, the album was complete. It was ready to be offered to the record companies. Radiohead knew that they had created something strong and unique, but they weren't prepared for the reception it was given. *The Bends* had taken about a year to catch on; music fans had fallen in love with what Radiohead was all about in slow motion. And *OK Computer* was a complex product; it would take time for the album to establish itself. Insisted Colin, "*OK Computer* isn't the album we're going to rule the world with. It's not as hitting-everything-loudly-whilst-waggling-the-tongue-in-and-out, like *The Bends*. There's less of the Van Halen factor" (Moran).

It is true that *OK Computer* didn't fit into the mainstream music scene, which had so slowly warmed up to *The Bends*. But like the music of REM, it didn't really seem to matter. The greatest test was whether Radiohead's latest offering was good enough to *redirect* the mainstream. It was.

I'M BACK TO SAVE THE UNIVERSE

10

Critically acclaimed albums are often consigned to obscurity. The bands who make them cling to the notion that people who enjoy fresh and challenging sounds will seek them out and buy them. But hope alone will not propel a record to number one on the *Billboard* charts, nor will it attract music buyers to a new sound, no matter how enthusiastic the reviews are. In recent times, bands like Belle and Sebastian, Yo La Tengo, Mogwai, Stereolab, and Sunny Day Real Estate have all released mind-blowing albums that will live in the hearts of those who hear them, but these bands are considered extremely lucky if their release exceeds sales of 100,000. Just compare the year-end lists of critics' favorites to an annual tally of top-selling albums. Of course, critics hail a range of popular acts as well: REM, U2, Nirvana, and even Oasis have been praised for their innovation or identified as the best of their class. Their albums have sold millions of copies because, while unique or even groundbreaking, they still have elements that render them accessible to the masses.

But could *OK Computer* elevate Radiohead to those exalted ranks? In the eyes of many people at both EMI/Parlophone and Capitol Records in the United States, the album did not have the feel of a popular hit. They had expected something quite different. Many of the songs they had wanted to release as singles weren't even on the album. Questions from both the fans and the record-company reps arose when *OK Computer*'s track listing was issued. Five much-loved creations had been completely passed over — "True Love Waits," "Lift," "I Promise," "Motion Picture Soundtrack," and "Man-o-War." These songs, by now widely available on the bootleg market, were beautiful, intelligent, accessible — and nowhere to be seen.

When I asked Ed about them, he gasped, leaned forward, and

asked, "How do you know those songs?" After I had explained about the underground recordings — a practice that the band neither promotes or denounces — he became more willing to talk about these unreleased tunes. "Didn't make the album," he said. "Didn't cut it. That could be it forever, or they might resurface later. There are a lot of bands who regurgitate old material, like 'Message in a Bottle' by the Police was written five years before by Sting, so there's no reason why we might not do 'Lift' or 'Man-o-War' later."

Commenting on the rumor that "Lift" would be the lead-off single from the album, Ed said to me: "People are strange, though. We thought ['Lift'] was a bogshite B-side and we were very happy to leave it off the album. There wasn't any stage where it was a key track for any of us. It is nice that people think that. Maybe we should reevaluate our thinking on that song." But how can a number that sounds so wonderful in the live setting sound like "bogshite" in the studio? "We don't work very hard at things," Ed claimed. "No, it's true. If there's something that could potentially be quite cool but it doesn't get it in the first five times of playing it through, we'll work on something that's musically more challenging. We would rather work on something like 'Flowers in the Hospital' than work on something simpler. Maybe 'I Promise' — we could have given that a bit more." "Last Flowers til the Hospital?" I asked. "That was one that we actually tracked and it sounded shite!" exclaims Ed.

And so the album was set with the 12 tracks band members had agreed upon, and the compilation was passed along to the record company. Disappointment about those excluded songs quickly evaporated. The Capitol people were slightly unhappy with "Electioneering," which they had expected to use as a single based on the way it sounded live, but they and their overseas colleagues threw their full support behind the record anyway. "We won't let up until they are the biggest band in the world," proclaimed Capitol Records president Gary Gersh (Irvin and Hoskyns).

When Parlophone managing director Tony Wadsworth got his hands on the album, he listened to it a few times and pronounced it the most influential album of the year. He was sure he had a winner on his hands. "Well, he's our MD, so he wants to sell some records," Ed joked to me; then he added, "He's a huge fan. Tony Wadsworth will, while we're sound checking, sit at the side of the stage because he used to be in a band himself. It's cool to get the MD of your label who has seen it all and done it all to be so enthusing about what you're doing. That's very nice of him to say." Wadsworth couldn't stop talking about the record or the band: "The unanimous reaction to this record is that it's something very special. The single is a brilliant piece of music. It might fly in the face of all the rules and conventions, but everything we've ever done with Radiohead that's worked has broken the rules. Because of that, they're going to change the acceptance to certain types of music" (Sexton).

Their album delivered, Radiohead was ready for a break. At least that was the plan. But instead of traipsing home to bed, Thom and Jonny plunged into an alluring project — a soundtrack for a movie titled *Velvet Goldmine*. The film, for which Michael Stipe sat in the executive producer's chair, was to be a look at the innovative bands that became the backbone of the glam-rock music scene of the 1970s — bands like the Stooges and the Velvet Underground. David Bowie had discovered these American acts in the late 1960s and returned home to England where he built a career with this new — and, at the time, strange — style of music.

The musical score attracted many musicians and bands, like Teenage Fanclub, Shudder to Think, Brian Eno, Grant Lee Buffalo, and Pulp. Two bands were created just for the project. The first was called Wylde Ratttz and included the likes of Mike Watt, Stooges guitarist Ron Asheton, and Sonic Youth's Thurston Moore, among others. The second band was Venus in Furs (taking its name from the classic Velvet Underground song), and it featured former Suede guitarist Bernard Butler, Roxy Music sax player Andy Mackay, former Grant Lee Buffalo bassist Paul Kimble, plus Jonny and Thom. Thom, Kimble, and Rhys Meyers all shared vocals as the group performed cover versions of Roxy Music songs for the film. They recorded quite a few tracks, three of which featured Thom doing an almost-perfect Bryan Ferry impersonation.

Meanwhile, Ed and Phil were thinking about the next Radiohead video. The band was determined that it be totally unlike any of their previous clips. So the pair headed off to Sweden to meet an intriguing director named Magnus Carllson. While in the studio, Radiohead members had always taken breaks whenever Carllson's animated show *Robin* came on, becoming enthralled by the story lines. The lead character, Robin, had many traits that reminded Thom of himself. In each episode, Robin would face various problems while his laid-back friend Benjamin glided through all kinds of difficult situations.

The interview with Carllson went well. Ed emerged from it convinced that a *Robin*-cartoon video of *OK Computer*'s first single, the six-and-a-half-minute "Paranoid Android," would be perfect. The director was initially hesitant to accept the job, but after listening to the song many times over realized that "it fitted [Robin's] lifestyle." (Morgan, "*ok* Animator"). Ed said to me, "It's very interesting the way this chap works. He has this office in Stockholm and it overlooks the street, and he sat in his office for eight or nine hours and played the track back to back relentlessly, just staring out the window, and he said that he kind of got into this trance that becomes almost like a mantra. And he looked at things going on in the street, and he sees things and they go inside of his head and they take a sort of a twist. He's very cool. It's frightening he does that stuff straight."

Having only the song to listen to — he was not sent a lyric sheet — Carllson managed to create a fascinating cartoon. Robin gets involved in a bar fight, is taken on a journey by an angel in a helicopter, and pays to see a woman's naked body. "I think it's the best video we've ever done," Thom announced, "and it's great because we didn't even do it. We weren't even involved" (Lee). The video, like the song, would be released in May to coincide with the launch of the band's promotional tour and interview schedule.

The fivesome reconvened in Ireland on 20 February at the *Hotpress* Awards, where they received their first award of the year: Best International Live Act. The prize was specifically for the stunning performance the band gave at the Olympia Theatre in Dublin on 26 July of the previous year. Sharing a table with Radiohead that night were members of u2. Chatting with u2 drummer Larry Mullen, Colin began drinking heavily. Approached by some press people who wanted the inside scoop on the new Radiohead album, he announced that *ok Computer* was "stoned Radiohead." The quote would come back to haunt him. "He lies all the time to these magazines," Ed told me with a smile. Colin laughed, "I didn't talk to them. They're drunk." Still, the incident got many people thinking that *ok Computer* was made in a haze of drugs, which, of course, wasn't the case. Colin later retracted his comment.

Together, the Radiohead boys turned the awards ceremony into a great drinkfest, gulping down the free Heineken. When it came time to accept their award, they made it to the stage but forgot to take the award with them when they left. After they finally got their hands on it they turned around and lost it again. They had to stay behind and search the theater after the ceremony was over.

A short while later, Radiohead's "Street Spirit" was honored at the *Music Week* Creative and Design Awards, taking top spot as Best Video of 1996. The awards ceremony, held on 14 April, also honored

Jonathan Glazer, who won Best Rock/Alternative Video for the "Street Spirit" promotional video. Yet the awards and credits had only just begun to stream in. The best Radiohead had to offer still hadn't been released.

Radiohead was set to kick off its 1997 performance schedule with a few concerts in Barcelona and a grueling three-day series of interviews. By this time, the secret lineup for that summer's Glastonbury Festival had already begun to leak out — at least the rumor mill was buzzing on the Internet and in the press. The word was that Radiohead would play Glastonbury on Saturday, 28 June. It would be the band's first British show to promote the new album. Before this, however, Radiohead was slated to play the Royal Dublin Showgrounds. Massive Attack and Teenage Fanclub were booked to open for them. The Irish venue had a seating capacity of over 35,000, and the concert sold out in three hours, proving that the Radiohead phenomenon had become larger than anyone — especially the band members themselves — had ever expected. And Thom was wrestling with the challenges of fame. "I can't see why we're doing these big gigs," he declared. "Thing is, whoever it is up there [on stage], it's not the person sitting here. It's a completely different state of mind, that you have to spend a long time getting into. I can't switch it on and off. Whenever the logistics of these big gigs are discussed, I just fucking freeze up. It's not something I'm emotionally capable of dealing with yet" (Doyle, "Party On"). In a *Q* magazine interview conducted before the release of *OK Computer* and before the final confirmation of the Glastonbury gig, Thom had elaborated on his anxieties. He was having problems sleeping. He knew how big and important Glastonbury was, and he was worried about what might happen when Radiohead took the stage (Doyle, "Party On").

In the weeks leading up to the release of the album, Colin once again talked to the press. This time, he was careful not to blurt out something he'd later regret. He tried to describe the new material to the band's eager fans, saying, "It was interesting listening to the album after it was finished. Every track sounds like a psycho-drama, you feel like you've been through the wringer after every song. It's like a roller coaster. You feel when you listen to the album you should have a safety belt" ("Radiohead: Vive la Megadrive!").

By the end of May, Radiohead seemed to have become the center of the musical universe. The signs were obvious. For one thing, the long-reluctant Radio 1 was now thrilled to play whatever single they cared to release — no matter how strange or somber. Bucking con-

Thom at the Tibetan Freedom Festival,
Downing Stadium on Randall's Island, New York

ventional wisdom, Radiohead elected to issue the six-and-a-half-minute "Paranoid Android" as a radio single. Stations responded by requesting a shorter mix. When it was clear that no such thing was forthcoming, stations all over the world put that extended cut into heavy rotation — length be damned. Radiohead could not be ignored. When the double EP hit the stores, the impact was phenomenal. "It went straight into the singles chart at number three in the UK and sold 94,000 copies in a week," Ed told me. "We've never done that before. And that just shows you — . . ." "The power of rock," interrupted Colin — ". . . how people can be duped," finished Ed.

But the song wasn't released just to annoy the likes of Radio 1. Representative of *OK Computer* in its entirety, it would serve as an excellent preview of the album. The video stations, however, when confronted with the Magnus Carllson clip, balked. Many music channels demanded an edited version. The video contains footage of a man wearing a spiked G-string cutting off all of his limbs and sinking to the bottom of a river. It also contains a shot of cartoon nipples. The stations didn't like the nipples. "You couldn't have really made any other kind of video to go with it," Phil explained to me. "I mean, anything else would have just looked really somber and really earnest. So you have to take what was really appropriate for the song. As it is it's going to be censored for certain stations, but their selection for censorship can be a bit bizarre. The bit to me where he is chopping off his arm, which is like the most disturbing part for me, that's fine."

At this point, Ed jumped in, saying, "Breasts, in America! For TV, you have to censor them." European stations are more flexible about such visuals, and Colin offered me this explanation: "I have a theory about this. It's the Catholicism, you see. It's the mother love, it's like very important so there's no problem with that in the Latin European countries like France, Spain, Italy. But for some reason, things are a little more uptight in other places." Ed interjected, joking, "It's weird, but in Miami they would love that video. Breasts, and way-hey. Hopefully, Latino MTV will be like, 'Yeah, give us more of that stuff. Come on, baby.' We'll get a special on Latino MTV where it's just a pair of breasts. That'd be cool, yes!"

But this time the band relented, and the video was altered slightly for certain stations. Soon enough, though, attention was diverted from the single by the album. When the reviews started appearing, people suddenly realized this wasn't just a new Radiohead album but a release that might very well change contemporary music itself. Jon Pareles reviewed *OK Computer* for the *New York Times*, comparing the album to the works of the Beatles and maintaining that Radiohead "combine[s] tender melody with troubled lyrics." *New Musical Express* reviewer James Oldham called it "age defining and one of the most startling albums ever made." He closed his perfect-score review with the words, "Truly, this is one of the greatest albums of living memory — and the one that distances Radiohead from their peers by an interstellar mile." *Mojo*'s Nick Kent announced that "Others may end up selling more, but in 20 years time I'm betting *OK Computer* will be seen as the key record of 1997, the one to take rock forward instead of artfully revamping images and song-structures from an earlier era" (Kent). And John Harris, who had praised On a Friday so long ago, wrote in *Select*, "in a world in which most music has become laughably 'instant,' *[OK Computer]* needs five or six plays before you even begin to understand it. . . ."

No matter what newspaper you opened, no matter where you were, you'd encounter *OK Computer* raves, and many critics pegged the release as one of the best of the year. Thom, who always found it so hard to accept praise at face value had this to say: "There's also an element of people hearing that a record is cool and feeling as though they'd better say they like it. I'm sorry, I'm quite cynical. There are records every year that are like that" (Hughes). But still, Thom was happy — not because of all those glowing reviews, but because one journalist who had really loved the album also felt that *OK Computer* was not the best that Radiohead could do. That, to Thom and the band, was a truly valuable compliment.

Fame had not gone to their heads. In fact, it wasn't unusual for band members to point out to their interviewers albums they judged to be much better than *OK Computer*, or even to criticize some of the songs on the album. Colin periodically noted that "Climbing up the Walls" was too overblown for his liking, and Ed remarked that while "Fitter Happier" was a great track it was probably not one that people would want to hear every time they listened to the album. "What we've always wanted to avoid is people getting out the skip button on the CD player or whatever," he told me. "But I believe that once people have heard the album in its entirety five times, that once it comes up to ['Fitter Happier'] the skip button will come out. Because it's very important as it sets the tone of the album. It's very important within the sense now, but I wouldn't want to hear 'Fitter Happier' late at night having heard the album six or seven times. I'd want to go on to 'Electioneering' after 'Karma Police.'"

In Barcelona the promotional stop was intense: when they weren't performing, band members were doing interviews or photo shoots. Journalists from all over the world had followed Radiohead to Spain and were eager to talk to them. Cameras flashed wherever they went and video director Grant Gee recorded their every move. The band had actually engaged Gee to make a video diary of all the major Radiohead events that would occur in the coming year. Gee was to follow them on their European travels, sit in on some interviews, and then shadow their world tour. The material Gee gathered would be edited down to make a video for Radiohead fans.

After leaving Barcelona, Radiohead played a Radio 1 *Evening Session* segment and appeared on *Later with Jools Holland*. Then it was back to North America for a small promotional tour that would also include an appearance at the second annual Tibetan Freedom Festival — held in New York City and organized by the Beastie Boys — to raise money for the Mariposa Fund. Before hitting New York, however, Radiohead landed in Toronto for a concert that sold out in 48 seconds, breaking that city's all-time ticket-sales record. On their way to the venue, Thom worked on a new song, tentatively titled "This Isn't Happening." The show that night was spectacular. Radiohead performed all of the tracks from their new album except "Let Down." Confronted by a flood of unfamiliar material, the audience still went wild. It was a triumph for the band.

At Downing Stadium in New York, they joined Michael Stipe, Eddie Vedder, Noel Gallagher, and the Beastie Boys for the Tibetan Freedom Festival. Stipe introduced Thom to a lot of celebrities and artists who were hanging out in the backstage area. The event was important to Radiohead on two fronts: first, because they believed in the cause it was intended to support; and second, because it demonstrated to them that they were now totally accepted by their musical peers. At last they could be themselves without holding back, without checking every word that came out of their mouths, and this was new and exciting for them. The band's set included two songs from *OK Computer*, "Lucky" and "Paranoid Android."

The cause of Tibetan freedom meant a lot to the band. Notes Thom: "We've tended to stay away from a lot of the political stuff, but I feel the Tibet cause is really important, because everyone knows what the Chinese are doing, but no one will just stand up and say 'You must stop!' All the governments have their hands tied by the fuckin' corporations. But musicians . . . we can give these corporations the big 'Fuck you!!'" (Hill). In the months prior to the New York performance, Thom had become engrossed by the Tibetan way of life, reading *The Tibetan Book of Living and Dying* by Sogyal Rinpoche. He had also begun meditating.

Two days after the festival, Radiohead played a New York club called Irving Plaza. This show, like the Toronto one, was filled with songs from *OK Computer*, and many in attendance that night have proclaimed it the best of the year. This assessment carries a lot of weight because it came from several of the band's peers: among the fans who came to see Radiohead at Irving Plaza were Madonna, Michael Stipe, Peter Buck, Bono, Liam and Noel Gallagher, and Marilyn Manson.

A week later, *OK Computer* was released in most parts of the world (though it wouldn't be released in the United States until 1 July). Not surprisingly, it debuted at number one in Britain. In Dublin, fans were so frantic to secure a copy of the album that shops were sold out of it by noon on the day of its release.

Meanwhile, Radiohead was still plugging away in America, promoting *OK Computer* by playing a special gig called the Weenie Roast for San Francisco's KROQ. The bill also included Blur and the Mighty Mighty Bosstones. But the British quintet were less than thrilled to be there. "We fucking hate these radio shows," says Ed. "They're not about music; it's about how many bands you can cram onto stage in six hours" (Freese). At the Weenie Roast, the band again played their new material; at this point, the album was due in American stores in about two weeks. After playing "Exit Music," Thom, aware that there was little reaction from the crowd said, "You really fucking hated that one, didn't you? You're all fucking mindless anyway, so you'll like this one." They launched into "The Bends." Later in the set, Thom was still angry with the audience — booing had erupted after his last comment — so he announced: "We're the first of the British bands today. We've come to show you how it's done. Here's another song to fill your barren lives, it's called 'Fake Plastic Trees'" (Cameron, "Notorious Pig").

Despite this low point, Radiohead returned to Europe feeling confident. They were about to play for over 35,000 fans at the Royal Dublin Showgrounds. Radiohead moved that crowd, proving once again that they were an astonishing creative force. Days later, they would headline the biggest festival in England — and possibly the world.

WHEN I AM KING . . .

11

Glastonbury is a three-day event that officially begins on a Friday late in June, though many fans show up much earlier to pitch their tents. In the past, Glastonbury had been a seamless combination of music, atmosphere, sun, and spirituality. This year, there was a tangible lack of that festival vibe. The weather conspired to transform the fairground area into a vast reservoir of mud. Conditions had become so bad that a handful of hugely anticipated acts were forced to cancel their appearances outright. The bands that did play were faced with the unenviable task of pulling the audience out of the mud and into the music. Most failed. On the first day, Friday, 27 June, even the Smashing Pumpkins and Prodigy were unable to elicit anything other than total indifference from the crowd.

As the festival pushed towards its midway point on Saturday, it became clear that Radiohead would be presented with an enormous challenge: to salvage singlehandedly an otherwise uninspiring and disappointing weekend. Backstage, band members were in a decidedly scattered frame of mind. They arrived only hours before their scheduled appearance, and quickly dispersed to different parts of the backstage area. Jonny and Thom were nowhere to be found. Rumors swirled that Thom was holed up in the tour bus fighting bouts of nerve-induced nausea. The others killed time by socializing in the beer tent and the campgrounds. Of them all, only Phil seemed genuinely unfazed by the looming prospect of playing to their largest audience yet — some 40,000 people.

As the eerie opening strains of "Lucky" filtered into the night sky, it became clear that this Radiohead performance was going to be one for the ages. Thom was in top vocal form, and although he appeared inhibited by the sheer size of the venue, there was no doubt he was up to the task. Delivering raucous renditions of "My Iron Lung" and the surprisingly well-received "Airbag," they loosened up, became fluid, glided deftly between new and old compositions.

Their set list contained songs that most bands wouldn't dare attempt in a festival environment. On the surface, the brooding balladry of "Exit Music (For a Film)" and the haunting, unearthly quality of "Climbing up the Walls" seem all wrong for an outdoor show with a festival audience. But somehow the songs worked, each one building on the momentum sustained by the last. The band was even inspired to deliver "Creep," a song that they had recently cut out of their concert lineup.

Like all legendary shows, this one had a single defining moment when the performance ascended into the stratosphere. During the instrumental break in a beautiful rendition of "No Surprises," someone off in the campgrounds ignited a small batch of fireworks. As the green and blue lights crackled and flickered in the sky above the stage, the awed crowd emitted a collective gasp, and when Thom began to sing the final verse the exhilarated fans joined in. Radiohead capped off the show with sobering versions of "The Tourist" and "Street Spirit (Fade Out)." Even after the band left the stage, the excitement in the audience remained palpable. For the first time that weekend there seemed to be a general consensus that history had been made.

Later it was revealed that the band had endured serious technical problems throughout their time onstage. In fact, there were moments when Thom could neither hear himself nor see anyone in the audience. Afterwards, he praised Phil for turning in one of the best performances of his life and for helping the rest of the band overcome a potentially disastrous PA-system malfunction. In light of all this, it was truly astonishing that the band had managed to deliver such a stellar and moving show. Backstage, Colin — visibly relieved — was already well lubricated with alcohol. He roamed around, stopping to chat with fans and musicians alike, all the while beaming like a proud father. Ed appeared tired, more subdued than his bandmates. As Phil calmly navigated the vast mud puddles that stretched between the stage and the tour bus, he graciously accepted the compliments of gushing onlookers. As always, he seemed genuinely serene in his tumultuous surroundings. Not surprisingly, Jonny and Thom were nowhere to be found.

The next day, Radiohead's Glastonbury performance was lauded by both the on-site media and people attending the festival. Not one Glastonbury review failed to declare Radiohead's performance the highlight of the event. No one, evidently, had noticed the difficulties the band had encountered while onstage. "The first four numbers were brilliant," remembers Colin. "Then Thom's monitors went, mine went, the lights went down, then the spotlights on the floor burned Thom's eyes out so he couldn't see anyone or hear anything. He started to make mistakes and miss cues and nearly walked offstage, but Jonny and Ed basically managed to talk him out of it . . . he didn't have any monitors for the encores, which is amazing. So it's really very mixed feelings. But if we'd done that a year ago, we would have definitely left the stage — and our career — in ruins. Ha ha!" (Dalton).

"This was their biggest moment in the UK and they did the business, but they just couldn't enjoy the moment," reflects Hufford. "The old karma police operate in a very queer way — you're never too big for a kicking" (Irvin and Hoskyns).

While the press touted Radiohead's Glastonbury performance as an event akin to the coming of the Messiah, the band didn't really have time to bask in the glory — they had to leave immediately for Germany and Belgium where they were booked for more gigs and festivals.

On 1 July, *OK Computer* was released in the United States, and though the album was considered a difficult work that would take most listeners a long time to grasp fully, it debuted on the *Billboard* Top 200 chart at number 21, a position much higher than *Pablo Honey* had achieved. Given the amount of hype and support the album had received, many were surprised that it hadn't done even better on the charts. But not Thom: "We didn't fit the fucking format. Fucking obvious. No Doubt fit the format, and we don't. That, to me, is a kind of bonus" (David Sinclair).

Setting up to tour North America in late July, Radiohead requested an opening band they all loved and respected — the impeccable Teenage Fanclub. This Glasgow, Scotland, combo had just released an album, *Songs from Northern Britain*, so both acts focused in on promoting their new CDs.

Only a couple of days into the tour, Thom departed temporarily to fulfill a musical obligation and realize a dream: he went to work with the brilliant DJ Shadow on a project called UNKLE, which was headed up by Mo' Wax honcho James Lavelle. The UNKLE album was to be a collaborative effort featuring the vocals of many artists, such as the Verve's Richard Ashcroft. The Beastie Boys' Mike D. Thom had been asked to sign on after Lavelle heard him mention that a Mo' Wax compilation, *Headz*, was a favorite of his. Lavelle wanted Radiohead for the project because he was a huge fan of *The Bends* — so much so that he did the Karma Sunra Mix of "Planet Telex" that came out on the "Just" single.

When Lavelle approached Radiohead about working on the UNKLE album, originally slated for a February 1996 release, Thom was extremely interested. He agreed to help out but couldn't devote any time in 1995 or 1996: he was all tied up with commitments for *The Bends* and recording *OK Computer*. It wasn't until July 1997 that Thom could get away briefly to Skywalker Studios (owned by filmmaker George Lucas), and there he and DJ Shadow worked on the track "Rabbit in Your Headlights." Thom provided the vocals and the lyrics, some of which he wrote on the way to the studio, while Shadow performed his magic and created the music. "Shadow is sort of a genius, and basically one of my heroes," said Thom only days after working on the track (Mulligan). The feeling was mutual. Shadow maintained, "That track was one of the most rewarding. After he did his vocal [Thom] ended up staying for two days tuning pianos and laying down extra bass parts. The track was built from the ground up" ("Manna").

Back on tour, Radiohead headlined venues across North America with seating capacities of between three and six thousand, and all shows were sold out. Their sets consisted almost entirely of *OK Computer* songs — including "Fitter Happier," which heralded their arrival onstage — and numbers from *The Bends*. Periodically, they pulled out a rare gem as an encore — "Maquiladora," "Banana Co.," or even one of the "Paranoid Android" B-sides, "Polyethylene." "Motion Picture Soundtrack" made the set list for a couple of shows, and occasionally the overplayed "Creep" crept into the lineup. "Sometimes I do have to justify ['Creep']," Thom remarked. "Sometimes it's karaoke, and I enjoy hamming it up, but some days it really means something to me" (Hendrickson).

Near the end of the North American tour, on 25 August, the second single from the album, "Karma Police," was released in most markets except the US. There, "Let Down" was on the radio and a video of the song was in the works. The "Let Down" video was to be half live action, half stop-motion animation, but the band was disappointed with the final product and vetoed its release. In fact, Radiohead had originally wanted to make videos for all the songs on the album, but as proposals for the clips poured in they realized that the cost of the project was prohibitive.

"Karma Police," however, was made into an unusual and highly effective video. Thom and director Jonathan Glazer shot it one June day on a deserted stretch of road three hours from London. In this Hitchcock-esque clip, we see the singer sitting in the backseat of a car that is pursuing a running man. Then the tables are turned. The man lights a match, which ignites a stream of gas leaking from the car. Much of the impact comes from the video's point of view — the viewer is placed in the position of the car's driver. Says Glazer: "The song's about retribution; so I wanted to do something that was a metaphor, the pursuer becoming the pursued, in a circular, Kubrick-like linear shot. I wanted Thom to seem as the story teller rather than the subject" (Morgan, "You"). "Radiohead are all about subtexts, and underbellies," explains the director. "Thom thinks about music in the same way that I think about film — he thinks it's a dialogue. That's why in the video he just sings the choruses, because the verses mean whatever we want them to mean" (Blashill). The double single set of "Karma Police" was released, debuting on the British charts at number 8. It contained interesting B-sides, including two remixes of "Climbing up the Walls," and "Meeting in the Aisle," an intriguing instrumental.

Radiohead's US tour came to a close with a *Late Show with David Letterman* appearance; they played their new British single. Then it was off to England to begin touring after a mere three-day hiatus. That sold-out British arena tour, marked by magnificent performances, was an unadulterated success. It included one very exclusive gig at the London Astoria for fan-club members. While everyone expected it to be a B-sides show, based on information leaked by the band, the set actually contained just a few rare tracks. Still, it was a treat for fans to hear "A Reminder," "Motion Picture Soundtrack," and "Banana Co." Thom even taunted the crowd by playing the opening chords of "Lewis (Mistreated)" before moving on to something else.

After the British tour there were a few dates in Holland, France, Belgium, and Germany. Now that their popularity was established in virtually every country, Radiohead was able to play larger venues and do fewer shows. The band once known for its killer tour schedules at last seemed to be taking things a bit easier. When some fans complained that their home venues were now being passed over, that Radiohead had become inaccessible, Thom was unimpressed: "What I think is fucking ridiculous is the way that you get to a certain point and people get extremely upset if you don't go and play in their country. I mean, extremely. And it's like blackmail, you know? So every time you do a record, you're blackmailed into going on tour for two years, which is bollocks. It's all part of the promotional marketing campaign, you see." Of the band's former nonstop tour routine, he adds, "I don't think there's anything worthy in going on tour for two years. You just turn yourself into a fucking maniac. And then you have to turn yourself back" (Harris, "Renaissance Men"). Besides, that amount of travel threatened to take a domestic toll. The lives of the band members had changed greatly since the club days of 1992 and 1993: Phil had been married for three years by this point; Jonny had also tied the knot; Thom was living with Rachel, his girlfriend of nine years; and Colin was living with his girlfriend. Time at home had become essential.

In November 1997, Radiohead set out for another tour of various arenas across England. Michael Stipe followed along, and later commented on how far the band had progressed. That progress was demonstrated by the way they'd taken control over the song that once seemed to be dragging them down: "When we toured with them two years ago, they played 'Creep' every night," said Stipe. "But now, they've taken that song back from the fans, and they've made it really beautiful" (Blashill).

The closing months of the year saw Radiohead inscribed on various top-album lists. Band members were amazed to see themselves ranked higher than Bob Dylan, Spiritualized, and the Verve, all of whom had released exceptional albums in 1997. And the work of bands from various countries was starting to reflect the influence of *OK Computer*; no matter what genre of music these bands played — even heavy metal — Radiohead's release had touched their hearts and minds. Still, the quintet didn't let it all go to their heads. Characteristically, they disputed some of the things that were said, especially about their degree of importance to the music world at large. "If we seriously thought that, we'd split up," insisted Ed, "because then you've achieved something, and it would only be destined to get disappointing afterwards. It's lovely when someone says that, but it doesn't register" (Dalton).

As for the label "art rock," which some critics had attached to Radiohead's product, Thom had this to say: "We write pop songs. As time has gone on, we've gotten more into pushing our material as far as it can go. But there was no intention of it being 'art.' It's a reflection of all the disparate things we were listening to when we recorded it" (Tony Sinclair). The band even rejected the adjective "unique." "We're just copying lots of records — and getting them wrong," explained Jonny. "The only skill we demonstrate is we recognize these accidents as being good when they are good" (Dalton).

123

Aside from making it onto top-five lists all over the world, Radiohead was named Band of the Year in several publications. One of the most impressive lists they landed on was that of the top-ten highest-selling albums of the year in Britain. Radiohead perched at number 8. In *Select*'s poll of the Most Important People in the World, based on input from music-industry people and musicians, Thom checked in at number 6.

Select asked the innovative instrumental dance-music composer David Holmes, to comment on Thom: "the John Lennon of our times," he replied. "I don't mean that in a personal sense, I mean it in terms of someone doing things that have never been done before" ("100 Most Important").

Emerging from this deluge of praise, Ed reflected on the positive side of remaining in the media spotlight: "We never wanted to be the biggest band in the world, we just wanted to know we could make another record and we can make one now — two actually. Now we can relax. We don't have to have all the answers in the next album" (Kessler). Despite the quintet's resistance, the music world had clearly recognized *OK Computer* as an achievement beyond the reach of most bands, a vivid testimony to the fact that even though rock and roll has been around for over 40 years it is still possible to push it forward, to create new and exciting sounds. Without ever intending to, Radiohead had challenged artists all over the world to rise to a higher standard. *Melody Maker*'s Robin Bresnark summed up the phenomenon: "if Radiohead aren't the best band on the planet, then Elvis is alive, rain is dry and lead floats."

WE ARE STANDING ON THE EDGE

12

The Beatles will forever and always be considered the ultimate purveyors of rock and pop. Many acts that sprang up during the same era are credited with infusing those genres with their innovative styles and unique sounds, but the Beatles' repertoire of both throwaway pop songs — most of which were number one on the charts — and thought-provoking and experimental compositions — remember *Revolver* or the band's self-titled album — has made that group a musical force that others can only attempt to touch. Those who pushed the boundaries made an impact on the legend: the Beach Boys' *Pet Sounds* greatly influenced the Beatles' *Sgt. Pepper's Lonely Hearts Club Band*. But the Beatles remain unsurpassed.

When *Q* magazine held a readership poll dubbed the One Hundred Greatest Albums in the Universe, many journalists around the world took note. Two things need to be kept in mind about this poll. First, it wasn't scientific: people could easily sway the results by voting more than once. Second, it was bound to reflect the fact that younger people generally don't consider innovative acts of the 1960s and 1970s when choosing the greatest albums or bands of all time; instead, they pick their current favorites. Many of the votes went to contemporary artists. Bands like Suede, Blur, and Oasis scored high; Prodigy's *Fat of the Land*, Oasis's *(What's the Story) Morning Glory*, and Nirvana's *Nevermind* made the top ten. Absent from those first ten positions were the Beach Boys, the Rolling Stones, and David Bowie. Pink Floyd's *Dark Side of the Moon* squeaked in at number 10, but other than that, only the Beatles represented music made before 1990. The Liverpool four made an amazing showing on the list: *Sgt. Pepper's* was number seven and *Revolver* number two. But they weren't the only band to have two albums in the top ten. There was also Radiohead.

Number six turned out to be the album that had taken 40 weeks to catch on with the British audiences, but by 1998 *The Bends* had become a revered artifact. Number one was *OK Computer*. The Greatest Album in the Universe. The Radiohead boys had to laugh — only in an anything-goes readers' poll could such a thing occur.

"The most important thing with our music is the way we play together," says Ed. "A lot of *OK Computer* is about the stage Radiohead got to [in 1996]. There's an understanding that goes on now; a lot of tracks were put down live with very few overdubs. But it was that whole thing about a band at a certain time being really able to play. We realized that we were playing the best we had in twelve years. And we will get even better" (Wylie).

Tony Wadsworth, who had elected to release "Street Spirit (Fade Out)" in January of 1996 to profit from all the attention *The Bends* had received at the end of 1995, decided to deploy this strategy again. "No Surprises" was released as a single in the third week of January 1998. And while it didn't hit the coveted number-one spot — Oasis's much-anticipated "All around the World" appeared the same week and edged it out — it did reach number four. No small feat. "No Surprises" was accompanied by a rather bizarre video: in it we see the upper portion of Thom's body being slowly engulfed in water until he's completely submerged, holding his breath for the musical solo.

The clip's director was good friend Grant Gee, who was still at work on the documentary. Gee says that the inspiration for the "No Surprises" video "came from two things. Firstly, *Blue Peter*, circa 1974: Singleton, Nookes and Purves biting their nails to the quick as they watched some minor escapologist in a Houdini scenario, locked, chained, straight jacketed and hung upside down in a tank of water. Secondly, a freeze from *2001: A Space Odyssey* [in which] HAL starts getting pissy with Bowman and won't open the doors to let him back on the ship . . . a huge close up of his face as panic starts to wash over it. It's the perfect image of anxiety and helplessness in the face of technology" (Morgan, "You").

As this single was released in Britain, Radiohead undertook an *OK Computer* tour in one of its most important markets: Japan. On this tour some notable changes were introduced. The band no longer walked onstage at the beginning of its set to the strains of "Fitter Happier"; instead, "Meeting in the Aisle" was used. Also, the B-side number "Pearly*" became a concert mainstay. Both songs were included on the tour EP that had recently been released in Japan, *No Surprises/Running from Demons*. Also, Radiohead played two really special songs in Japan. One was a B-side of the *Paranoid Android* EPs, "A Reminder." The other was a new one that the band claimed had no official title, referring to it as "Nude." It tells the story of a man who has no trouble achieving sexual satisfaction but who feels guilty about it. Some fans had actually named the tune "Big Ideas (Don't Get Any)," but the band never adopted that title. Thom performed it with an acoustic guitar accompaniment on 23 January at the Akasaka Blitz in Tokyo.

Wrapping up their Japan exploits, Radiohead flew to New Zealand and Australia, two countries they hadn't played since June of 1994. For two weeks, they delivered the goods to sold-out-arena audiences throughout this territory. It was an exciting time for everyone involved.

While the band was on the road, the awards and honors continued to roll in. Radiohead was nominated for three Brit Awards: Best Group, Best Album, and Best Single for "Paranoid Android." As it turned out, the extremely successful *Urban Hymns* by the Verve cleaned up. Radiohead was consoled by two prestigious Grammy Award nominations: Best Alternative Album and Best Album. The Grammies, while mandated to reward the best that the music industry has to offer, has acquired a reputation in recent years for being primarily sales-driven. But many of the 1998 nominees were, in fact, commercially unsuccessful in the US market: witness *OK Computer* and Bob Dylan's *Time out of Mind*, both of which made the Best Album category without having to compete with the likes of multimillion-selling Puff Daddy.

The 1998 Grammy Awards ceremony was a scene of triumph for the grizzled and legendary Dylan. He snared the Best Album award, but in the Alternative category Radiohead was victorious, beating out David Bowie, Prodigy, Björk, and the Chemical Brothers. The Verve were ignored at this event. "The fact that we won a Grammy was really, really unexpected," says Ed. "I think [it] is testament to the fact that the record has moved quite a few people and has touched people, and people have got it" (Pearlman).

The Grammy success elevated Radiohead to a higher echelon; they went global, their image appearing in all kinds of publications — from financial rags to mainstream music magazines — the world over. People who had somehow failed to hear the name Radiohead were now reading all about the band and their accomplishments. Band members and their management agreed that the time was ripe for Radiohead to tour North America again. They needed to capitalize on their accelerated notoriety. Tickets went on sale a month before the scheduled April dates. The venues they would play were the largest they'd ever had to fill, and fill them they did: all of the shows sold out, and many in record time. Radiohead also covered cities on this tour that they had either never played before or hadn't played in years. Cities like Dallas, Texas, and Salem, Oregon, threw out the welcome mat.

Before embarking on this tour, Radiohead took a five-week-from-touring break during which they tried to record a song titled "Big Boots" for the upcoming *Avengers* movie soundtrack. Originally part of the Leckie sessions back in 1994, the song had been played by the band live in 1995 under the title "Man-o-War," but they had never honed it to the degree that it could be recorded. Now, try as they might, the band just couldn't bring "Big Boots" to completion. "No we ditched it . . . because we were so messed up and we went in, tried to do the track, but we just couldn't do it," explains Thom. "It was actually a really difficult period of time. We had a five week break and all the shit was coming to the surface. It was all a bit weird . . . I mean we went in and tried to do this old track that we had . . . and it just wasn't happening at all. It was a real low point after it" (Pinfield).

Fans who had attended a Radiohead show the previous year noticed that band members seemed tired on the North American tour — not as into performing as they had been. But their set list harbored a few pleasant surprises. First, "Nude," which the quintet still referred to as an untitled song, was offered up as a full-band song. Both Thom and Jonny manned the keyboards for this number (which they covered occasionally, not at every gig), and some parts that in Japan had been sung were now replaced with instrumentals. Another song, the one that Thom had begun writing in Toronto back in June of 1997 under the working title "This Isn't Happening," was included in the set as well; its title had mushroomed to "How to Disappear Completely and Never Be Found." A lyrically poignant piece about longing to escape a situation that you don't want to be in, the song clocked in at over seven minutes (but considering the original running times of "Just" and "Paranoid Android" we can assume that if this song appears on a future CD it may be in a similarly condensed form).

Around this time, Thom was making news on his own. Drugstore's record-company problems had been worked through; the band had secured a new record deal and were now set to release their long-awaited sophomore album, *White Magic for Lovers*. The first single, released on 20 April, was "El President," the song Drugstore had recorded with Thom. A video for the track was in the works, and Thom had agreed to participate. One video director floated the absurd idea of having Monteiro and Yorke appear naked in the clip. All concerned laughed at the suggestion, but Thom, in the mood to stir things up, proposed that they announce it to the press. The Internet was soon awash in rumors; fans chatted about the prospect of seeing Thom's naked butt on their TV screens. The actual video, released with the single at the end of April, features both Thom and Isabel fully clothed. The double EP came out on 20 April and debuted at number 20 on the British singles charts before falling off, but this was great for Drugstore — the outfit hadn't released anything in Britain in quite some time.

Then, on 1 April, Thom found himself in the public eye again. Radiohead was preparing to play Los Angeles. World-famous KROQ radio asked Thom to do an early-morning interview with two of its DJs. One of them, named Bean, kept harping on Thom's bad eye, joking about how it never looked straight. Thom blew off Bean's cracks at first, but the DJ wouldn't leave it alone. The interview featured two live performances, acoustic versions of "Creep" and "Fake Plastic Trees." At the close of "Creep," Bean pointed out that Thom could look off in two different directions at once. Thom lunged at the DJ and an on-air fight broke out. The station received hundreds of calls that day, and once again Radiohead Internet sites lit up — this time with reports that Thom had been hospitalized. Fans fretted that the LA show at the Universal Amphitheater, which had sold out in five minutes, would be cancelled. But it was 1 April. "Thom" was just an impersonator, and his "live" performances were actually tapes of previous shows. April fools? Radiohead declined to comment.

By the end of the tour, Thom was telling his audiences that he really wanted to go home. Since 1992, Radiohead had spent virtually every day on the road or in the studio. Every member of the band was running on empty. Winding things up with two nights at New York's Radio City Music Hall, Radiohead returned to the UK, but this didn't mean they left the limelight. First, only a day or so after the tour ended, a new Radiohead EP was released in North America titled *Airbag/How Am I Driving?*. It debuted on the *Billboard* chart at number 56, impressive considering it was composed entirely of B-sides from various British EPS and there were no videos for the lead song. Then, in mid-May, Radiohead won two Ivor Novello Awards for songwriting. These honors are based entirely on quality, not sales figures. Radiohead walked away with Best Contemporary Song of 1997 for "Karma Police" and Best Song Musically and Lyrically for "Paranoid Android."

Jonny was recognized for his playing once again, this time in *Guitar World* magazine. His "Paranoid Android" solo placed at number 34 — only 14 spots below Thom's first music idol, Queen's Brian May — in *Guitar World*'s Top 100 Guitar Solos of All Time roster. Describing that winning solo, Jonny remarks, "It was something I had floating around for awhile, and the song needed a certain burn. I don't usually have stockpiles of riffs lying around, but this happened to be in the right key and at the right speed, and it fit right in" (Bowcott et al.). Nigel Godrich, OK Computer's engineer, seconded *Guitar World*'s endorsment. He, too, was astounded at Jonny's talent: "I can't think of anyone else in my generation who has come to their instrument and left it as a different instrument. The way that Hendrix changed the way that people looked at guitars, likewise Jonny does things that people will imitate in ten years. Stylistically he does something original which is no mean feat in this day and age. But Ed's a great player too and Thom is a fantastically gifted guitarist, but you don't notice because he's got that amazing voice" (Kessler).

Throughout early 1998, Grant Gee had been editing the Radiohead tour video, titled *Meeting People Is Easy*. The official release date for the documentary was set: the end of November in the UK and early 1999 in North America. It featured footage from a few dates on the OK Computer tour, including concert clips from Paris, New York, and Tokyo, and it began with the Barcelona press fiasco. The documentary also previewed some new, unreleased material. "The real challenge is trying to make a rockumentary about a rock band that doesn't feel like it's a 'rockumentary,'" says Gee of his finished product. "Radiohead deserve more than that. I wanted to make a documentary that fits the imagery of OK Computer" (Thompson).

In the middle of June, Radiohead participated in the third annual Tibetan Freedom Festival. But this time around, their rising profile in the US — OK Computer had just gone platinum — ensured them a much more prominent role in the show. At the festival, journalists asked various performers why they were supporting this cause so adamantly, especially when the Chinese government had stated that all bands participating in the festival would be banned from playing in China forever. As one of only two British acts at the festival — the other was Pulp — Radiohead had to field a range of questions concerning the British stance on the Tibet situation. "In 1959, Britain was one of the countries who could have said something and didn't, so there's a definite moral obligation for the British people to be represented here," replied Thom. "It's very much a global issue, anyway.

And because the Tibetan struggle is a non-violent struggle, it shames the global community's ineffectiveness as a peace-keeping unit" (Lestor).

The 1998 festival was of unique importance not only because it was in Washington, but also because it culminated in a Capitol Hill rally mounted to pressure President Bill Clinton into raising the Tibetan cause on his state visit to China the following week. The plight of the nonviolent Tibetans, their suffering at the hands of the government of China, continued to disturb Thom; the momentous events of his own life hadn't diminished his sense of urgency. "One of the most important issues, as we near the end of the 20th Century, is that killing has become an arcade game," he declared. "This is the responsibility of everyone on the planet. By doing nothing, you condone the violence. We're involved in this event because of its principle of non-violent resistance. This shames governments and corporations involved in China. We establish relations with the Third World because we want to make things cheaply. We want our trainers cheap and then we walk away. If we carry on doing this at the end of the 20th Century, then God help us. Rock stars generally don't have the moral high ground, but in this case, they do" (Grundy). Phil agreed with Thom's views, saying, "[The Tibetan] non-violent aspect is important. There are so many conflicts around the globe today that could be more effectively addressed with a policy of non-violence" (Lestor).

Radiohead was set to take the festival stage on Saturday, 13 June, the final act of the day. Then the weather took a bad turn. One member of the audience was struck by lightning — which left her in critical condition — and ten more were also seriously injured. Organizers decided that things were getting out of control and cut the Saturday performances short. Radiohead, REM, and Sonic Youth were rescheduled for the Sunday, but the Oxford five were primed and ready; they were determined to play *somewhere* on the Saturday. An intimate Radiohead show was quickly arranged at the 9:30 Club in Washington, with Pulp as the opening act. Admission was free for the first 800 people who showed up with Tibetan Freedom Festival ticket stubs. By all accounts, the band delivered an incredible performance. "How to Disappear Completely and Never Be Found" made it onto the set list that night, but the highlight was when Michael Stipe joined Radiohead to sing "Lucky."

Early on Sunday afternoon, Radiohead finally took the festival stage. Stipe helped them with "Lucky" again, and the rest of the eight-song set included mainly *OK Computer* cuts — at the very last minute, however, Thom slid the crowd-pleaser "Creep" onto the roster. Later in the afternoon, during REM's monumental performance — which included a few tracks from their as-yet-unreleased album — Thom returned Stipe's favor. He sang lead vocals on "Be Mine," a tune from REM's 1996 album *The New Adventures in Hi-Fi*. Thom later returned to the stage to sing backup on "E-Bow the Letter," because Patti Smith, who had sung backup on the recording, was unable to make the show because of the weather. At the rally on Capitol Hill, Thom played an acoustic version of "Street Spirit (Fade Out)."

Then, at long last, Radiohead took a vacation. Immediately, their fans began to toss rumors around on the Internet that a new album would appear by the end of 1998, but the band nixed the suggestion, explaining that they would not return to the studio until November 1998. Of course, rumors also arose about what songs would be featured on the fourth album. Not surprisingly, speculation centered on some of the songs that were left off *OK Computer*. The band isn't completely secretive, offering some hints about what fans might expect down the road. Ed promises that future recordings will be "more diverse. I think we'll go down the 'Airbag' route more often, using loops a lot, but then there'll be other stuff where we'll be a really simple, close-miked five-piece band." But don't anticipate 12 "Airbag"-esque songs: Ed is quick to note, "We've got this whole ethic of wanting to try new things out. We don't want to do the same thing twice, certainly not within the space of a couple of albums. We want to go to new places musically" (Kessler). Thom tends to evade all such questions with humor. The next album, he says, "will sound like it was done a bit quicker, heh heh! I think it will be more direct. And obviously it will be happier, fitter, leaner and generally look like it's just stepped out of a salon, heh heh!" (Dalton).

In the meantime, however, fans haven't had to do without a fresh Radiohead fix. Along with the Drugstore track, Thom's collaboration with DJ Shadow, "Rabbit in Your Headlights," came out in the UK in late August (and a month later in the US), part of the highly acclaimed UNKLE album *Psyence Fiction*. The album debuted on the British charts at number one, propelled to such heights by the fact that it was new work from DJ Shadow and James Lavelle and that a string of high-profile artists appeared on it. The first single released from the album was "Rabbit in Your Headlights," and it appeared on 13 October.

Velvet Goldmine, to which Jonny and Thom both contributed, was released in late September in Britain. It contained five tracks by

Venus in Furs, three of which feature Thom's vocals. Despite the mixed reviews the album received, Thom's Bryan Ferry impression on these Roxy Music covers is considered brilliant — a clear testament to his incredible vocal talents.

In the fall of 1998, Radiohead was once again honored at the MTV Awards. This time, they garnered four nominations: Best Group, Best Alternative, Best Direction, and Best Cinematography for the "Karma Police" video. While Radiohead just couldn't compete with the likes of such American mega-sellers as the Backstreet Boys, Green Day, Madonna, and Fiona Apple, achieving those four nominations was quite a feat for the band. Those honors symbolized the total acceptance these former one-hit wonders from a foreign land had attained in the vast American market.

* * *

With new material on its way, many now think that "Nude" will get an official title and be the lead-off single, or that "True Love Waits" wasn't tossed out and will one day grace CD players around the globe. But no one knows what Radiohead will choose to do, and for every piece of perfection that may be rejected for being too overblown or too uninteresting to work on another classic will be recorded.

"Where do we go from here?" asks Thom in "The Bends." Where *does* Radiohead go from here? When their first North American single became an overnight hit, critics predicted they'd quickly fall back into obscurity. When they released *The Bends*, fans and critics alike were astonished at the sophistication and complexity of the work, and claimed the band would never be able to top it. But *OK Computer* changed all that. The possibilities are endless. Radiohead may go anywhere, and we'll be following close behind them on their mission to "save the universe."

the
r a d i o h e a d
s o n g b o o k

The following is a compilation of every Radiohead song ever released — and a few that have not been. I've included Radiohead's own explanations of the tracks, culled from interviews, but for most of those songs that were never defined by the band in print I've offered some possible interpretations. I've also included some anecdotes about the recordings, when available. But, of course, each song has a special meaning for each person who listens to it; no single interpretation can ever be definitive.

This section may also be used as a collector's guide to rare tracks. Tracks are listed in the order of their original release date, not the order in which they were written. However, remixes or live versions are discussed in the main entries, regardless of release date.

Early Unreleased Songs

Give It Up

An early demo recorded on a cassette along with "What Is That You Say?" and "Stop Whispering." This tape helped On a Friday convince Chris Hufford and Bryce Edge to produce their *Manic Hedgehog* demo.

The Chains

Taking advantage of Jonny's ability to play the viola, this song was the group's attempt to sound like the Waterboys.

Rattlesnake

Jonny claims that "Rattlesnake" "had a drum loop that Thom did himself at home on a tape recorder with bad scratching over the top and kind of Prince vocals" (Doyle, "Party On"). The song has also been described as "countrified ghetto rap" (Thompson).

What Is That You Say?

A "feedback frenzy," is how Jonny describes this track (Doyle,

"Party On"). Recording it made him realize how much he wanted to work with Thom.

Jerusalem and Everybody Lies through Their Teeth

Both of these songs are about living in Oxford. Reflecting on his hometown's influence, Thom has said, "It's such a weird place and it's very important to my writing" (Ronan).

Released Songs

1991

I Can't

Altered slightly from the demo-tape version for inclusion on *Pablo Honey*, this is a simple tune about lacking confidence. The band has rarely played it live.

Nothing Touches Me

One of the earliest tracks from the On a Friday days, this song appears only on the *Manic Hedgehog* cassette, though it is fairly easy to obtain on the tape-trade market. Thom decribed the composition in an early interview: "[It's] based on an artist who was imprisoned for abusing children and spent the rest of his life in a cell, painting, but the song is about isolating yourself so much that one day you realize you haven't got any friends anymore and no one talks to you" (Ronan). The painter to whom Thom is referring was also the inspiration for the computer art he created while at Exeter.

Phillipa Chicken

Available only on the *Manic Hedgehog* tape, this jangly pop song is about not wanting to fall in love. The number was removed from the band's live set in late 1991 and hasn't been played since.

Thinking about You

Initially part of the *Manic Hedgehog* demo, this touching love song focuses on the experience of being left behind by someone who has achieved fame, and on the relief of masturbation. It exposes Thom's ability to offer very different but realistic perspectives on issues. In its original form, the tune was very heavily guitar-oriented with a much faster tempo than the acoustic version found on *Pablo Honey*. This rocking version also appears on the *Drill* EP and *Itch*.

You

A love song of an obsessive nature that first appeared on the *Manic*

Hedgehog demo. This version was included on the *Drill* EP. For *Pablo Honey*, the song was rerecorded and some of the lyrics changed. Performed live, the song is an excellent showcase for Thom's incredible vocal abilities; he holds one note throughout the guitar solo.

1992

Prove Yourself

The first official single by the band, released only in the UK, this song looks very seriously at suicide. Unfortunately, like most songs that become popular, the meaning tends to get lost in live performance: band members were shocked to witness hundreds of kids singing "I'm better off dead" night after night. The version found on the *Drill* EP is a demo; a much better, clearer recording was used on *Pablo Honey*.

Stupid Car

Thom's first musical take on driving is about a car accident he survived in 1987. "Stupid Car" appears only on the *Drill* EP in its original form. Later, it was rerecorded as part of the *Volume* compilation series for *Issue Seven* and dubbed Tinnitus mix. The airy sounds of this mix blow past your ears, evoking the driving experience; vocals come in at a lower level. This version is much easier to find.

Creep

The big hit single. When it was first released, Radio 1 found it too depressing, and so after having been aired only twice it was taken off the station's playlist. The song has been analyzed by many people, and theories of what it's about range from Thom's terrifying childhood to Thom's deceased wife. Thom, however, was not an abused child, and he's never had a wife. At certain shows, Thom offers a partial explanation of the song. Written while he was at Exeter, he says, it tells the tale of a drunken student who tries to get the attention of a woman he's attracted to; in the end, he lacks the self-confidence to pull it off. This song has been released in a few versions: the original contains the word "fucking"; the radio edit (on which the F-word is replaced by "very") appears on several compilations and is a bonus track on the American version of *Pablo Honey*. The "Pop Is Dead" single also includes an intense live version of "Creep" that opens with Thom's explanation of how the track could have been a hit; it was recorded before Tel Aviv or America had even heard the song. Yet another live version came out on the Netherlands *High and Dry Live Package,* where you can experience Thom holding the word "run" for an incredibly long time. Lastly, there is a beautiful acoustic version recorded at San

Francisco's KROQ in 1993, which has appeared on various EPS and singles. Next to the original, this version is most definitely the best.

> Thom: "I don't write happy songs. Besides, emotions aren't defined as happy and sad, are they? Unless you're in advertising" (Barringer).

Lurgee

In this song about lost love, Thom sings that he is much better off without the other person in his life. "Lurgee," unlike most other songs from this period, found its way into the band's live set in 1998. One of two songs recorded with Chris Hufford at Courtyard Studios, it was selected for inclusion on *Pablo Honey*. The same version was used as a B-side for "Creep."

Inside My Head

Among the first songs Radiohead wrote after signing with EMI/Parlophone, "Inside My Head" deals with the experience of being picked up by a major label and leaving part-time jobs behind. Thom notes that the song is also "about getting in a car and ramming the shop where I used to work. I just wanted to do that so badly" (Jennings, "Jeepers Creepers!"). This tune was originally intended to become a single, but "Creep" was chosen instead. The live version on the reissue of "Creep" is far superior to the original studio take.

Million $ Question

Yet another song written right after the band got signed, this one looks at the corporate mentality — fat bankrolls, big promises. "Million $ Question" also seems to reflect Thom's feelings of doubt at this time, closing with the sample that says, "I just think maybe I'm making a mistake." The track was a live favorite in 1992 and 1993, but Radiohead took it out of their set a few months after the release of *Pablo Honey*. Of all the band's rare early B-sides, this is definitely a standout.

1993

Anyone Can Play Guitar

"Grow my hair / Grow my hair I am Jim Morrison / Grow my hair / I wanna be wanna be wanna be Jim Morrison." These now-famous lines got many critics and fans wondering. What did it all mean? Thom explains: "I just ranted that verse the day after I saw The

Doors film. That film really wound me up, really upset me. It was like [Morrison] was some sort of Arthurian legend or something" (Muretiche). Jonny played guitar with a paintbrush on this cut. The live version, a B-side to *Just* CD2, is far superior to the *Pablo Honey* track.

Faithless, The Wonder Boy

"I can't put the needle in . . .": band members insist that this line is not about doing drugs. Instead, says Thom, it's about getting revenge. A B-side for "Anyone Can Play Guitar," this track was a live favorite for much of 1993, but was rarely played thereafter.

Coke Babies

Radiohead's shoe-gazer-esque song is lyrically simple, based largely on the word "easy." The music is also simple, but features some mesmerizing sounds. The song is not a fan favorite. At the end of the track, humming can be heard—it's Colin singing along, unaware that the tape was still rolling. This is one of the band's most difficult songs to find, available only on the deleted "Anyone Can Play Guitar" single.

Jonny: "All Thom's songs eventually come down to how he's feeling" (Malins, "Scuba Do").

How Do You?

An in-yer-face song from the debut album, "How Do You?" was part of the band's live set during 1993. The number seems to be directed at an enemy, though the band hasn't offered a specific explanation. Listen closely to the guitar solo and you'll hear a sample from the Jerky Boys' "Pablo Honey," which would have been taken from bootleg tapes.

Stop Whispering

Written as a tribute to the Pixies, an important influence on Radiohead at this time, "Stop Whispering" clinched the band's relationship with the management team of Hufford and Edge. Chris Sheldon remixed it for a United States release; that version features strings and has a slower tempo. The best version of this song, however, is the live one. Thom adds a few lyrics to the ending. A live version can be found on the *High and Dry Live Package*, which contains a closing "fuck you."

Ripcord

This lyrically intelligent look at the music world is about "signing [to a label], having lots of money and absolutely no idea what the fuck to do with your life" — so said Thom at the band's 1993

Gothenburg, Sweden, show. Thom's skill with metaphors is evident as he explores the control a record company wields over its artists. The song was a live favorite throughout the early part of the band's career but was dropped from their set list around mid-1995. A live version of the song, a B-side to the "Pop Is Dead" single, was recorded at a Town and Country Club gig in February 1993, when the band supported Belly. It contains these lyrics, added after the second chorus: "They can kiss my ass!"

Vegetable

This song has never been explained by the band, but likely deals with personal problems Thom had with friends when Radiohead was signed. It ponders the reactions of his pals to his newfound success. "Vegetable" was a live favorite, though it exited set lists around the summer of 1995. The live version that originally came with the "Creep" rerelease is also available on the Japanese CD *Itch*. Definitely worth the price of the CD!

Blow Out

Jonny's favorite *Pablo Honey* track and the band's closing song of choice for many of the early shows, "Blow Out" is one of Thom's more personal songs about low self-esteem. On the reissue of the *Creep* EP, a remix of this track appears as a B-side. The remix opens with Thom singing over a simple guitar line. This version has a much faster, feedback-induced ending than the album version. The remix is difficult to track down, but you'll be glad you did.

Pop Is Dead

Bound for *Pablo Honey*, this song was actually left off the album and instead released as the band's final single of 1993. Thom describes it as "a kind of epitaph to 1992. Hence the lines, 'Pop is dead / [Long live pop] / Died an ugly death by back catalogue'" (Paphides). Band members seem to concur that this is a very weak track, deserving of the scathing reviews it received. Nevertheless, it's a catchy rocker with clever lyrics and explosive guitar lines.

Banana Co.

While most of the band's 1993 songs have been dropped from their live set, this beautiful number is still periodically covered. "Banana Co." originated on the "Pop Is Dead" single as an acoustic track from a radio session Thom did in 1993; then a studio version made it onto the benefit compilation *Criminal Justice: Axe the Act*. This new recording, with electric guitars, was also used as the B-side on the second part of the "Street Spirit" release.

Yes I Am

Reflecting an attitude Thom has held since childhood — he's the underdog who wants to show up the people who always put him down — "Yes I Am" sticks it to all those phonies who are suddenly your best friend when you make it big. The song was featured on the reissue of "Creep," made after the band had found success in the United States.

1994

My Iron Lung

Written the day Radiohead was forced to pull out of the Reading Festival in 1993 due to problems Thom was having with his vocal cords, this song comes off very bitter. But as it progresses, "My Iron Lung" seems to drive out Thom's anger about how the band's music was largely ignored — aside from "Creep." Thom has admitted in interviews that he is very proud of this song's lyrics; he felt he had perfectly captured the essence of what he was writing about. A few live versions have been released, and all are as intense as the original, though the tempo of some versions is quicker than the one on *The Bends*. The chorus on the live recordings (not given in the lyric sheet) is a bit easier to figure out: "The headshrinkers / They want everything / My Uncle Bill / My Belisha beacon."

The Trickster

An inspiring song for all budding guitarists. Its instrumentation, as much as its vocals, make it such a fan favorite. Like many other tunes from the *My Iron Lung* EP, "The Trickster" has only been played live on a few occasions, which is unfortunate.

Punchdrunk Lovesick Singalong

The song at first seems to deal with a war-torn scenario, but then comes the chorus containing the lines, "A beautiful girl / Can turn your world into dust." This moving composition deserves more attention. The band has played it live only a couple of times; luckily one of these occasions was at the Melkweg in Holland at the end of 1994, so the song was included on the *High and Dry Live Package*. This version is just as beautiful as the original studio recording. Colin claims that the real reason the band plays the song live so rarely is because he never properly learned the bass line.

Lozenge of Love

Titled after a line from Philip Larkin's poem "Sad Steps," this song was debuted during an acoustic set at the FNAC Auditorium in Nancy, France. It's another example of a Radiohead track where the lyrics were changed radically from their original form when the song was recorded for the EP. This beautiful acoustic number contains touching lyrics about not always being there for others, but sometimes needing others to be there for you.

Lewis (Mistreated)

With its infectious guitar riff, this song features Thom offering advice to a friend who just doesn't have the ability to be what he thinks he can be. Although "Lewis (Mistreated)" is another popular B-side, Radiohead doesn't play it live.

Permanent Daylight

This song was part of the band's mid-1993 live set as an instrumental, and Thom explained that it had been offered for a soundtrack but ultimately rejected. It was, at this time, much shorter than it is on the *My Iron Lung* EP.

You Never Wash Up after Yourself

A personal song finished in just one take, this track was one of the few released in 1994—95 that John Leckie did not help to produce. Instead, it was done with Jim Warren at the band's makeshift fruit-farm studio.

1995

Thom: *"The downside [to* The Bends*] was that everything I wrote had significance to it"* (Hendrickson).

High and Dry

A song that came out of Thom's Headless days (his Exeter band), this track was kicking around for a long time. Radiohead recorded a demo in 1993, but everyone agreed at the time that it didn't sound like a typical Radiohead song. The tape was rediscovered during the *Bends* sessions, and Leckie pushed to have the song on the album. He succeeded. The 1993 demo version was used for the album, produced by the band and Jim Warren. "High and Dry," which has been introduced as being about, or dedicated, to Evel Knievel, is about people who will do anything, including risking their own lives, to achieve fame.

Planet Telex

"Planet Xerox" was this song's original title, but because Xerox was a copyrighted name, Radiohead changed it to "Planet Telex." The only song written in the studio during the *Bends* sessions, it was recorded one night when the band returned to the studio after drinking a lot of wine. Thom did the vocals lying down, completely drunk. This is the most frequently remixed song in Radiohead's

141

roster; different versions appear on singles, promotional releases, and compilations. The album version is guitar-oriented, and so is the live version on *Just* CD2.

The Hexadecimal Mix by Steve Osborne has an extended opening, but overall the song drags on too long and doesn't provide the buildup necessary to make it a dance-floor hit. The Hexadecimal Dub by Osborne is, unsurprisingly, much like the mix, though slightly more experimental with keyboards and less guitar-oriented. This version is superior to the Hexadecimal Mix. The LFO JD mix by LFO is centered on a metallic drumline and the only vocals are the occasionally repeated words "You can force it." The track doesn't really go anywhere and becomes annoying, proving that remixes can sometimes be a sad waste of B-side space. The Karma Sunra Mix by UNKLE is the best remix of this song. In this very experimental version, which integrates varying sounds and musical styles, you can hear Thom breathing for a minute before he sings. All vocals are used, and the samples at the end enhance the track. The Depthcharge Mix, with an airy opening and a lack of precision between the beat and the vocals, is an unusual but intriguing version. It is very long and moves in different directions to maintain interest. The Trashed Mix by Alien Beatfreak has a thick drumline throughout and a periodic guitar riff. It is devoid of vocals, and without the guitar it would be impossible to tell that this was "Planet Telex." Still, it's a great track. Your best bet, however, is to see the band live, as they will never reproduce such a phenomenon on CD.

Maquiladora

An amazing rock song that stands up to the band's edgier material from their early years, this gem is for all the *Pablo Honey* lovers who may have had a hard time getting their head around *The Bends* when it was first released. With brash guitar lines, a wonderful solo, and classic lyrics — including the line "Useless rockers from England" — this is yet another entry on the list of great songs relegated to B-side status.

Killer Cars

Thom's second song on a driving theme, this one deals with the fear that every time we venture out in our cars we may be killed. Originally intended for release as one of the singles from *The Bends* during the initial recording sessions, the song actually debuted in the band's live set in 1993. "Killer Cars" has appeared in three forms. The first was the live acoustic version from the 1993 Chicago Metro show, which appears on the "Creep" reissue 12" and the Japanese CD *Itch*. This very passionate performance renders the tragic lyrics all the more moving. The second version appears as a B-side to the *High and Dry/Planet Telex* CD2, a straightforward guitar-oriented interpretation with mesmerizing percussion and a blistering guitar closeout. Last is the Mogadon Version, which is much mellower than the first studio release of the song. A newscast has also been blended into the mix. This version contains a similar ending to the previous one.

The Bends

This track was initially introduced as being about "knowing who your real friends are and when they're going to come to your gigs." Thom soon simplified this to "knowing who your friends are." The song reflects Radiohead's sense of humor; it contains many ridiculous lines about the CIA and the Marines.

Of the opening, Thom says, "The sound at the beginning comes from this caterwauling mayhem outside this hotel in the States. There was this guy training these eight-year-old kids, who were parading up and down with all these different instruments. The guy had this little microphone on his sweater and was going: 'Yeah, keep it up, keep it up.' So I ran out and taped it" (Malins, "Scuba Do").

So many interviewers asked about the line "I wish it was the sixties" that Thom starting to regret having written it: "I really do wish I never wrote that fucking song — it's become the bane of my life. Hundreds of journalists, asking — every single fucking interview, asking — 'Do you wish it was the sixties?' No! I don't wish it was the fucking sixties — Levi's Jeans wish it was the sixties — I certainly fucking don't" (Morlin).

The demo version, available only on the *Long Live Tibet* compilation, has loud guitars at the opening, lo-fi production, a slower tempo, and lifeless vocals with voices singing slightly different lyrics. This version is interesting simply because it is unusual, but it will just make you love the album version even more.

Fake Plastic Trees

A song written for the world of mass marketing and mass consumption. Many versions of "Fake Plastic Trees" are available, including the single from *The Bends* and an acoustic version on the CD single part 2, which also appears on the *Clueless* soundtrack. Live versions can be heard on *Het Beste Uit 10 Jaar 2 Meter Sessies*, the *Tibetan Freedom Concert* triple-CD set, and the MTV *120 Minutes Live* CD. This song was the band's proudest moment, and it remains a live favorite for very obvious reasons. No matter what version of "Fake Plastic Trees" you manage to get, you won't be disappointed.

Bones

Yet another song (like "My Iron Lung") that reflects Thom's obsession with poor health, this is perhaps a product of the physical

143

tribulations of touring. The song looks at Thom's fear of growing old and becoming physically incapacitated.

(Nice Dream)

This song revels in a happy-life fantasy, but concludes that it can be nothing more than a "nice dream." Heard at the end of the track are selections from an Arctic-sounds tape of John Leckie's. The demo version, available on the compilation *Volume 13*, is mainly an acoustic number featuring organ and strings. This version also contains the original lyrics of the song. The second verse chronicles a sweet fascination: "I'm the sweet man / Made of chocolate / Your licorice eyes will enrapt me . . ." While the album version is lyrically superior, this one is still worth a listen.

Just

Here Thom tells the story of how he once had a narcissistic friend he was compelled to elude. Musically, "Just" is considered the most complex track on *The Bends* album, and it proves beyond a doubt that Jonny's guitar playing is original and superb. A live version of this track is available on the double-CD compilation *Evening Sessions: Priority Tunes*; while it captures the intensity of the song live, the original remains the best.

Bullet Proof . . . I Wish I Was

One of the songs that prompted reviewers to believe that Thom had some serious personal problems, "Bullet Proof" actually has a more universal meaning, which invites the listener's personal interpretations. This is truly one of the best songs in the band's roster, and one of Thom's own favorites. The instrumentation was created by Jonny and Ed; they recorded their guitar noises without listening to other layers of the cut. These guitar-sound tracks were then put together and mixed with the rest of the song. An acoustic version, also released on the second part of "Fake Plastic Trees," is every bit as delicate and gorgeous as the *Bends* version. The song was debuted in France in 1993 with different lyrics.

Black Star

For Thom, this song is special. Although he has never offered an explanation of it, throughout 1995–96, when the band played it live, he did introduce it in various ways — declaring, for instance, that the song is about sex. The lyrics probe the destruction of a relationship and touch on sex with a third party.

Sulk

One of Thom's earliest creations, this song was inspired by a ruthless and unexplained killing spree conducted by a lone gunman in Hungerford, England, in 1987. Although its original concluding lyrics were "Just shoot your gun," these were changed when the song was recorded in late 1994. This was because the death of Kurt Cobain was still weighing heavily on people's minds while the Hungerford killings were not; Thom chose to change the lyrics so that no one would think the song was about the late Nirvana leader. "Sulk" is rarely heard live: the band played it in concert a few times in 1994, even less often in 1995, and never again after that.

Street Spirit (Fade Out)

This song was written in 1993, around the same time as "My Iron Lung." If "Creep" is Radiohead's American hit, this is the British equivalent. Laced with Ed's absolutely perfect arpeggios, the track has a mesmerizing quality that links it to the work of Stereolab. With lyrics about feeling like a very small person in an intimidating world, this fan favorite is memorable and timeless. We can only hope that Radiohead will retain it in the live set. A few other versions of this song have been released — two stripped-down acoustic ones and another from the band's *Evening Session* from September 1994. Like "Fake Plastic Trees," this exceptional song is perfect in all of its released versions.

Thom: "If I knew exactly what I wanted to say, then I wouldn't write the song" (Reid).

India Rubber

This very experimental B-side is based largely on Phil's heavy drumming. The lyrics wander all over the place, but there are still some memorable lines. The song closes with laughter, blending after a moment with the sounds of people talking and generally making noise — a party atmosphere.

How Can You Be Sure?

When this track was first heard on radio, in 1993, Thom noted that the title was only tentatively "How Can You Be Sure?" and that he hoped to change it. This never happened, though on the first Japanese issue of *The Bends*, which includes two bonus tracks, the song was called "When I'm Like This." This acoustic number, with backing vocals by Dianne Swann, is similar to "Fake Plastic Trees" in the way it builds as it progresses. The song is yet another look at relationship problems. The version on the *Nowhere* soundtrack is identical to the *Fake Plastic Trees* B-side version.

Lucky

From Ed's sweet, tingling, opening riff, the rest of "Lucky" was generated. "I remember fiddling around in the sound check," he says. "[W]e were in Japan — and putting together a different pedal order and actually hitting the strings above the nut on the headstock. The pedals that I did it with, and the delay that was going on. It was one of those moments — 'Yeah, this is pretty cool'" (Wylie). From here, "Lucky" was made into what the band considers a "happy" song, or at least as happy a song as they are capable of creating. A band favorite for some time after it entered the live set, the number ranks among the best Radiohead have ever recorded. An identical version, which can be found on both the *Help!* compilation and the *Help!* EP, also appears on *OK Computer*. This wasn't the plan: the band did try to remix the track for the third album but found they couldn't improve on it. Two live versions have been released — a live B-side to "No Surprises" recorded in Florence, and a superior live take from the band's special performance for *Launch* magazine. The latter was recorded in an empty Washington, DC, hall during Radiohead's 1997 tour, probably while the sound check was in progress; the acoustics are perfect.

1996

Talk Show Host

One of the best B-sides ever recorded by any band, "Talk Show Host" presents Radiohead exploring the trip-hop style. The song recalls Portishead's debut album, *Dummy*. The original version, on the *Street Spirit (Fade Out)* CD1, is the most guitar-driven of the versions released. The band has never articulated the song's meaning, but the number does contain some of Radiohead's best lyrics, especially: "You want me, well fucking well come and find me / I'll be waiting with a gun and a pack of sandwiches." The next version released was the Nellee Hooper remix on the *William Shakespeare's Romeo and Juliet* soundtrack, which differs from the original in that it includes various backing sounds and far less guitar, giving it a mysterious feel. The most unusual version is the Black Dog remix, in which the instrumental part and the vocals are played at different tempos than they are on the original — it's hard to sing along with. This version is very wild, and when the acoustic guitar comes in, the track takes on a magical quality. The best version, however, is the live take, with Jonny's added keyboards and a wonderfully long guitar jam at the end.

Bishop's Robes

Despite Thom's assertion that the song has nothing to do with the headmaster of Abingdon School, he has also said on other occasions this adversarial figure from his past *was* the inspiration for "Bishop's Robes." This exceptional track has periodically made it into the band's live set.

Molasses

The weakest track to come from the first, 1995 recording sessions with Nigel Godrich, "Molasses" pushes Colin's bass guitar to the forefront. Unfortunately, like the substance it's named after, it doesn't really go anywhere. The confusing lyrics don't help.

1997

Paranoid Android

"It really started out as three separate songs and we didn't know what to do with them," explains Thom of the creation of this six-and-a-half-minute epic. "Then we thought of 'Happiness [Is a Warm Gun]' — which was obviously three different bits that John Lennon put together — and said, 'Why don't we try that?'" (Bowcott et al.).

After being asked if the song was about the Fall of the Roman Empire, Thom adopted this explanation, but other band members have likened the lyrics of the track to those of "The Bends." On one level, the lyrics are absurd; on another, they're quite serious. During the band's 1996 live sets, when they were opening for Alanis Morissette, the song ended with a very long Hammond solo courtesy of Jonny, drawing it out to the eleven-minute mark. The live version from Glastonbury is an amazing version.

Polyethylene (Parts 1 and 2)

This opens as a short acoustic number (part 1) before blowing up into an incredible rock song. The lyrics perpetuate Thom's health fixation, but the actual meaning of the song isn't clear. "Polyethylene" was a welcome addition to the band's live set on a few occasions during the 1997 and 1998 tours.

Pearly*

The obscure lyrics of this song deserve pondering. The version available on the *Paranoid Android* CD1 and the US *Airbag* EP is considered the original, and the remix is available on the *No Surprises/Running from Demons* EP. The latter has clearer production values and a slightly louder guitar at the beginning; Jonny plays a different ending on the guitar. Both versions open with both Phil and Ed on drums. "Pearly*" made it into the band's live set on the latter half of the OK *Computer* tour.

A Reminder

"That song was written in one of those days off you have on a tour where you literally, all you can do is sit in your hotel room cause there's nothing," explains Thom. "It [was] a Sunday, and it's somewhere near Hershey, I got no idea where we were and there was just nothing to do at all. And I had this idea of someone writing a song, sending it to someone and saying, 'If I ever lose it, you just pick up the phone and play me this song back to remind me'" (Douridas). The song is brilliantly performed and captures the idea Thom expresses perfectly. It also contains a sample from a train and opens with Czech voices. Definitely one of the best songs in the band's roster.

Melatonin

Based first on the keyboards and then a drum line, this track never caught on with fans. It's an interesting piece, though — the lyrics take the perspective of parents watching over their son. Melatonin is a hormone produced by the body to regulate sleeping and waking cycles, but its production decreases with age. A hormone supplement has now been formulated that compensates for this decrease.

Airbag

Originally titled "An Airbag Saved My Life," a headline that Thom read in an Automobile Association manual that came in the mail, the song is "about the wonderful, positive emotion you feel when you've just failed to have an accident; when you just miss someone and realize how close it was and stop the car and just feel this incredible emotion" (Sutherland, "Return"). The title is also a play on the 1983 Indeep song "Last Night a DJ Saved My Life."

The song reflects the influence DJ Shadow has had on Radiohead, as the band made the track with a drum loop based on a three-second sample of Phil's drumming. "Airbag" was an excellent choice for first cut on OK Computer: it opens the proceedings with the chorus, "In an interstellar burst / I am back to save the universe." The live version released on the UK No Surprises EP captures the song's intriguing and oppressive atmosphere.

Subterranean Homesick Alien

Originally called "Uptight," which is how Jonny referred to it in its early stages, the song pays homage to Bob Dylan's "Subterranean Homesick Blues." It deals with alien abduction and stems from two incidents in Thom's life. The first occurred at Abingdon School, when he was assigned an essay question that went something like this: "If you were an alien from another planet arriving on Earth, how would you describe what you saw?" (Clapps). The second incident occurred when Thom was driving down a country road and hit a bird (which he believed was a pheasant). He stepped out of the car and at that moment began thinking about alien abduction.

"Subterranean Homesick Alien" was first played acoustically back in 1995 during radio broadcasts. It wasn't until OK Computer was made that the organ was added. Many fans prefer the earlier versions to the album version, and the earliest version was released on the compilation *Rare on Air: Volume 4*, which sees Thom and Jonny playing the song with acoustic guitars; both verses are sung together and the song closes with the chorus. This version is a treat, and a great addition to any Radiohead fan's collection.

Exit Music (For a Film)

While on tour with Alanis Morissette in September of 1996, Radiohead was sent the last half-hour of Baz Luhrmann's film *William Shakespeare's Romeo and Juliet* and asked to write a song for the closing credits. Band members were impressed by the clip, and Thom wrote this song for the movie. At first he attempted to use lines from Shakespeare's play as lyrics, but finally ditched this idea.

The moment in the film when Claire Danes (Juliet) holds a Colt 45 to her head was the actual inspiration for "Exit Music." Thom also had the 1968 version of the film in his head: "I saw the Zeffirelli version when I was 13 and I cried my eyes out, because I couldn't understand why, the morning after they shagged, they didn't just run away. The song is written for two people who should run away before all the bad stuff starts. A personal song" (Harris, review).

Let Down

This track was recorded in the ballroom of actress Jane Seymour's mansion at 3 A.M. It closes with computerized sounds created by zx Spectrum computers, which all the members of Radiohead owned in the 1970s. Jonny explains what it's all about: "It's like when Andy Warhol said he enjoyed being bored. It's about that feeling that you get when you're not in control of it — you just go past thousands of places and thousands of people and you're completely removed from it" (Sutherland, "Return").

Thom: "We're a mess. But it's a great mess, a glorious mess . . ." (Reid).

Karma Police

"It was a band catchphrase for a while on tour — whenever someone was behaving in a particularly shitty way, we'd say, 'The karma police will catch up with him sooner or later,'" says Jonny. "It's not a revenge thing, just about being happy with your own behaviour" (Sutherland, "Return"). Thom laughs, "This is a song against bosses, fuck middle management!" (Steele). "Karma Police" was debuted back in 1996 during the Alanis Morissette tour. Thom sang the line "This is what you'll get" an octave higher than he does on the album, with brilliant results. Ed was the one who originally suggested they do a song based on the catch-phrase.

Fitter Happier

Many people mistook the computerized voice on this track for that of physicist Stephen Hawking. The strange voice was, in fact, created by Thom on his Mac computer. He recorded it one night in an isolated area of the rehearsal space that the band had set up. Ed told me about it: "Thom basically had this checklist, like a nineties checklist if you like, and he had written it out. There is a bit of him playing the piano, [which was] in the rehearsal room. He was very drunk one night, which you can tell by the sloppy playing on it, and he just played out this little melody and stuff. He was very anxious that it wasn't him saying [the lyrics] — this voice is neutral. By the computer saying it, it doesn't become a bit of pretentious art-wank, it's something neutral in the way that the computer stumbles over words and doesn't get the pronunciation or the inflections right." Adds Thom: "The reason 'Fitter Happier' exists is 'cos of mental background noise. Some days you're in a disturbed state and it moves to the front" (Harris, "Renaissance Men"). The track was used as an entrance song for the band on their 1997 tour.

Electioneering

Thom describes this song as being about preaching to others through a microphone. He uses the metaphor of a politician selling his party platform to critique the live promotional shows Radiohead was doing to sell its music (Sutherland, "Return"). In its original, 1996 live form, the song ended on a very catchy note with Thom repeating the line "Doin' it all." Many fans were surprised and a little disappointed at the final version that made ok Computer.

Climbing up the Walls

This is first track in the band's repertoire to be described as "scary." It relies heavily on strings, but not in the conventional way. The string section, covered by Jonny alone, features 16 different violins playing quarter tones apart from each other.

The audience's cue that the band is about to play this song live comes when Jonny pulls out a small radio and begins tuning it to different stations. During the band's sound checks, Jonny locates classical-music or news-oriented local radio stations, and uses these — never rock stations — to execute "Climbing up the Walls."

Two remixes of this song exist, and both are truly unique. The first remix, the "Zero 7" by Henry Binns and Sam Hardaker, is a very mellow, string-induced, trip-hop version that only briefly brings in the original melody. The final screaming by Thom is placed low in the mix; television sounds are played over top. The "Fila Brazillia" mix also strays far from the original. This version uses a few different types of beat, a little organ, and some other unusual sounds; Thom's vocals go over top. While both remixes are worth listening to, neither re-creates the horror that emanates from the original version.

No Surprises

Thom introduced this song to his bandmates and the members of REM on the REM *Monster* tour. It was 3 August 1995, in Oslo, Norway, and they were all gathered in a dressing room. The lyrics have been changed since then, but they originally told the story of a man who has become fed up with the way things are working out for him and is having problems with his girlfriend. Two lines from this version are, "He was sick of her excuses / To not take off her dress when bleedin' in the bathroom." Preparing to record the song, Thom altered those lyrics, but the meaning remains essentially the same. Aside from the fact that it features a glockenspiel, this track has a simplicity that proves Radiohead's ability to create a basic song with straightforward lyrics and make it fit smoothly into an album as complex as *OK Computer*.

Ed: "I don't think the fun side of Radiohead shines out from our albums" (Dalton).

The Tourist

"The Tourist" was written by Jonny, who, explains Thom, was "in a beautiful square in France on a sunny day, and watching all these American tourists being wheeled around, frantically trying to see everything in ten minutes" (Harris, review). Jonny was shocked at how these people could be in a place so beautiful and so special and not realize it because they weren't taking the time to just stop and look around.

Meeting in the Aisle

For this track, Radiohead explored a new avenue — it's an instrumental piece. While the band has yet to play it live, "Meeting in the Aisle" was used as an entrance song (taking the place of the much-loved "Fitter Happier") for the band's 1998 shows. The track was programmed by Henry Binns and Sam Hardaker.

Lull

A very simple song featuring Jonny on the xylophone, "Lull" is personal in nature. It sees the singer inexplicably losing control, for which he is apologetic. With the lyrics "The stress and the tension

/ I'm in a lull," and then later, "I'm sorry that I lost control," this song reflects a trait Thom admitted to having: he often loses his temper without really knowing why he has become angry.

1998

Palo Alto

Palo Alto, California, is home to many of America's large corporations, including Xerox and a few computer companies. When the band played there in March 1996, they were given several tours of these temples of economical and technological advancement. Thus, the song is about the "city of the future" — the motto of Silicon Valley, which is situated in Palo Alto — and ponders the friendly attitude of the people the band members met there; Thom greets those people in the chorus. This is a great guitar-rock number, but, like most Radiohead tracks, it is incorporates some fascinating background sounds and is musically complex.

How I Made My Millions

Thom wrote and sang this song at home using his four track, but when he took it to the band as raw material they decided that it should stay as it was. The version on the B-side to "No Surprises" is, therefore, the original four-track recording. While Thom was creating the song, his girlfriend, Rachel, was in the kitchen putting away the groceries or making supper, and the noises she made can be heard in the background. As for the song's meaning, it has never been disclosed by the band, and the lyrics are almost unintelligible. Since Radiohead has achieved success by putting out records that make people question what Thom is saying and what he really means, the title couldn't be more suitable.

New Unreleased Songs

(While none of these songs have been released to date, a few were expected to appear either on *ok Computer* or as B-sides to the singles from that album.)

Last Flowers til the Hospital

This song was part of the *ok Computer* recording sessions, but, as Ed told me, "It was one that we actually tracked and it sounded shite." The song, as described by the band, had elements of David Bowie in it, and was a favorite of Colin's, who explained that while he knows all band members must be in agreement before a track is used on an album, he was still upset to see this one left off.

True Love Waits

A beautiful acoustic number that has only been played once, at the Luna Theater show in Brussels in December of 1995. This performance features Thom on acoustic guitar and Jonny on keyboards, and is filled with brilliant lyrics about needing a certain person in your life. Two lines that stand out for many are: "I'm not living / I'm just killing time." Whether this song will ever make it onto a record is unknown, but it would be a pity if more people don't get to hear it — this is a Radiohead treasure.

Motion Picture Soundtrack

Thom absolutely adores this tune, and expected it to make it onto *OK Computer*; unfortunately, the band decided not to include it. However, they did perform the song on a couple of occasions during the *OK Computer* tour, demonstrating that the piece hadn't been consigned to oblivion. It's hard not to shed a few tears when Thom sings to his woman, "I will see you in the next life."

Lift

Lift is a British term for elevator, and this song is about being stuck in one. "Lift" is also the first song in which Thom actually referred to himself by name, taking the voice of a person who is trying rescue "Thom." Despite the rumors that this number would be an *OK Computer* single, Ed told me that the band had never considered it. Played regularly in 1996, the song was identified by most reviewers as the best new song they had heard in sets that also included "I Promise" and "Electioneering."

I Promise

An REM-influenced, crawl-back-on-your-knees-and-beg-forgiveness-for-screwing-up song, "I Promise" was written around the time that Thom was basing many of his songs on the outside world and what was happening to others. So it isn't necessarily about him. The song was played regularly during the 1996 tours, but then vanished from the set list and never resurfaced.

Big Boots

The band played this song a few times in the fall of 1995, and at that time referred to it as "Man-o-War." They didn't play it after this, but in early 1998, when asked to contribute a song to the soundtrack for *The Avengers*, offered a tune titled "Big Boots" — "Man-o-War" under a new name. Unfortunately, due to road fatigue and time constraints, band members were unable to come up with a satisfactory finished product, and so they decided to pull out of the soundtrack project.

Thom: "To me, pop songs will always be the most powerful way of saying anything. I've no intention of doing aural soundscapes, or whatever. It's not gonna happen" (Irvin).

Nude

This song is actually introduced by the band as an untitled piece, but on Web sites it is often referred to as "Big Ideas (Don't Get Any)," a title the band has never officially accepted. "Nude" is the title that appears on the band's set lists, though the song has never been referred to elsewhere by this name. The piece features both Thom and Jonny on keyboards (though when it was first played live — in Tokyo, on 23 January 1998 — there was just Thom on an acoustic guitar), and it is as gorgeous and mysterious as both "Motion Picture Soundtrack" and "True Love Waits" as far as the unreleased material is concerned. Influenced by the notion that we live in a man's world, a place where men can get whatever they desire, the song also explores the guilt that men feel when they commit certain acts, like cheating on their partners.

How to Disappear Completely and Never Be Found Again

One of the band's newest songs, "How to Disappear" debuted during the band's North American tour in April 1998. Thom began writing the song in June 1997 while Radiohead was in Toronto, calling it "This Is Not Happening." It is a fairly lengthy piece, clocking in at almost seven minutes, but Radiohead has the tendency to edit down original versions before recording them ("Paranoid Android" and "Just" are two examples). So, if the song makes it onto the band's fourth album or if it pops up as a B-side, it may be in a very different form. Lyrically, this is a beautiful piece about wanting to escape from the life or the experiences that you face. Musically, it is a showcase for yet more of Ed's compelling guitar sound effects.

Life in a Glass House

Written by Jonny, this number is mentioned in a *New Musical Express* article by Ted Kessler, who witnessed the band performing it during a sound check. They never played the song live but did work on it during various sound checks so that they could get more comfortable with it, a method Radiohead has used for many songs. Kessler maintains that "Life in a Glass House," which is about having problems with a good friend, is "as doomed as 'Perfect Day' by Joy Division" (Kessler).

Collaborations

Wish You Were Here (Thom with Sparklehorse)

This track was originally released as part of a special EMI compilation titled *Come Again*, which features several current artists covering older songs. If you're a fan of Sparklehorse, this cover of the Pink Floyd classic is an essential addition to your collection. As far as Radiohead fans are concerned, though, this track will likely be of interest only to those bent on completing their sound libraries down to the very last item. Sparklehorse lead singer Mark Linkous sings the entire song; on a hotel-room phone, Thom sings a very soft backup — no words at first, just humming. He also switches on the TV heard in the background.

El President (Thom with Drugstore)

This excellent song was written by Drugstore. They sent it on to Thom, asking if he thought it was good enough for him to provide vocals for; Thom responded by asking if they thought he was good enough to sing it. "El President," which deals with the death of Chilean President Salvador Allende, was laid down in 1996 in the studio, but Drugstore was experiencing label problems (their label, Go! Discs, was going bankrupt), and so the song was not released as a single until April 1998. Thom did supply the vocals but somehow didn't sound right, so he was called back into the studio to record them again. The final product may very well display Thom at his vocal best.

Rabbit in Your Headlights (Thom with DJ Shadow)

This six-and-a-half-minute epic was one heavily anticipated collaboration. It opens with a beautiful piano line, and its lyrics, written by Thom on the way to the studio, are as touching as those used in many Radiohead songs. Thom also plays guitar and synth. As the track progresses, DJ Shadow's brilliance surges to the fore; an array of sounds and a mesmerizing drum line are blended in. As the song comes to a close, Thom holds a few notes for an amazingly long time. High hopes for this track were clearly fulfilled.

An EP of remixes was released, and all of these new versions are brilliant. The song was wildly reconstructed by the Underdog, Robert Del Naja (3D from Massive Attack), and David Axelrod. The Underdog mix uses an acoustic guitar, strumming a completely new rhythm but working perfectly with Thom's vocals and the string arrangement. When the drums take over the song, sending things off in a new direction, the track attains new heights. The 3D Reverse Light Mix is perfect in the sense that in it you can still hear the qualities that make the song a DJ Shadow/Thom Yorke creation, but 3D also makes the mix sound like something belonging on a Massive Attack album, which is terrific. Both the Underdog and 3D mixes come with instrumentals. The final mix on the EP is the Suburban Hell Remix by Axelrod, and it's the best on the EP. As a cello plays alongside Thom's vocals, the listener is drawn into this string-filled version — a brilliant take on an amazing song.

2HB / Ladytron / Bitter-Sweet (Thom and Jonny with Bernard Butler, Clune, Paul Kimble, and Andy Mackay)

These three Roxy Music covers all appear on the *Velvet Goldmine* soundtrack. Thom perfectly impersonates Bryan Ferry. Hearing "2HB," fans will be surprised at the deeper tone of Thom's voice, but the singer proves capable of handling the lower range just as easily as he does the falsetto. The explosive guitars at the end of the song, courtesy of Jonny and Bernard Butler, demonstrate just what an incredible team these two make. On "Ladytron," the woodwind instruments, lashing guitars, and sexy tone of Thom's voice will make you wish that the entire soundtrack consisted of Yorke-sung, Venus in Furs versions of Roxy Music songs. The soundtrack's best song is "Bitter-Sweet." Here Thom sounds a bit more like himself in the slower piano opening. When he explodes into the very glam-rock, domineering chorus, he raises his voice to an all-out scream. Pure beauty.

Baby's on Fire / Tumbling Down (Thom and Jonny with Bernard Butler, Clune, Paul Kimble, Andy Mackay, and Jonathan Rhys Meyers)

These two songs were also performed by Venus in Furs, but on the tracks listed here Jonathan Rhys Meyers sings. From "Baby's on Fire," a Brian Eno number, this incredible group of musicians tries to create an energetic, intense track, but their efforts fall a bit short. The insane guitar grinding in the middle comes courtesy of the two Radiohead members and Butler, and while this is great, Meyers's vocals weaken things. In this extremely catchy cover of "Tumbling Down," which was originally done by Steve Harley, Meyers's voice is almost perfect. The guitars are traded for pianos, recorders, and cellos.

Live Cover Songs

With the exception of the Roxy Music covers that Thom and Jonny collaborated on for *Velvet Goldmine* and the cover of Pink Floyd's "Wish You Were Here" that Sparklehorse put out with a minimal amount of assistance from Thom, Radiohead has never been interested in recording cover songs for tribute albums. Jonny told me why: "We got asked to do a James Bond thing and very silly kind of tribute albums, but we shy away from that. Usually it's stuff that we

don't listen to, like we were asked to do one for Kiss. Or if it's someone really good like Nick Drake or whatever, you kind of don't feel
worthy enough to do it." Performing covers live, however, is a different story.

Rhinestone Cowboy (Glen Campbell)

Ed is a country-music fan and really likes Glen Campbell, so it's not
as surprising as it may seem that the band did this song live. They
performed this in France in June of 1993. Thom hit all of the notes
perfectly, and the boys even played guitar with a country twang
that would make Campbell proud.

Nobody Does It Better (Carly Simon)

Thom once introduced this song to an LA audience by calling it "the
sexiest song that was ever written." Radiohead has played it live
many times, even as recently as 1998. Thom's voice is a superb fit
for the song. It was originally written by Carole Bayer Sager and
Marvin Hamlisch and was sung by Carly Simon for the James Bond
film *The Spy Who Loved Me*.

Sing a Song for You (Tim Buckley)

This one comes from Thom's favorite Tim Buckley album,
Happy/Sad, which was released in 1968, and Thom has performed
it twice, on his own. The first time, he did an acoustic version for a
1993 concert on San Francisco radio station Live 105; the second
time, he played it at the 1994 Reading Festival.

Union City Blues (Blondie)

Radiohead played this Blondie tune only while doing *The Black
Sessions* in France, right before *The Bends* was released.

Wonderwall (Noel Gallagher)

Thom and two members of the Posies, Ken Stringfellow and Jon
Auer, only partially performed this Oasis song. They launched into
"Wonderwall" as a joke on Canadian radio's *CBC Real Time* on 22
March 1996. After about a minute of playing — Thom was singing
and forgot most of the words — the trio abandoned the effort.
Thom claims Oasis doesn't mind such "tributes."

Related Songs Not By Radiohead

Radio Head (Talking Heads)

This song is featured on the 1986 Talking Heads album *True
Stories*, which is a compendium of pop-oriented tracks that form

the soundtrack of the movie of the same title, produced by the band's lead singer and songwriter, David Byrne. The Talking Heads were a favorite of all Radiohead members; they thought this was a great track from an album that didn't offer many other interesting cuts. The song's chorus is, appropriately, "Oh Radio Head / The sound . . . of a brand new world."

Pablo Honey (Jerky Boys)

Band members first heard this song on a bootleg tape obtained by Chris Hufford. It was later released on the second album by the Jerky Boys, *Jerky Boys 2*. Radiohead titled their own debut album after the track because it contains the motherly voice of a crank (Jerky Boy) caller speaking to her "Pablo, honey." Thom, after all, claims that Radiohead members are "mother's boys" (Cavanagh).

the
radiohead
discography

This annotated list features all of Radiohead's albums and singles. While most of the singles cited were released only in the United Kingdom, I've also included some special releases from other countries. Since naming every compilation that Radiohead has contributed to is beyond the scope of this book, only those compilations that contain a nonalbum track or a B-side are included.

ON A FRIDAY

Manic Hedgehog Demos (October 1991)
Cassette
I Can't / Nothing Touches Me / Thinking about You / Phillipa Chicken / You

Virtually impossible to find nowadays since the edition was so limited, this cassette was independently released and sold at the Oxford record shop Manic Hedgehog. Meanwhile, Colin worked at Our Price, its competition. The price tag on the cassette was £3.

159

RADIOHEAD

UK Singles

Drill EP (5 May 1992)
CD / 12"/ cassette
Prove Yourself / Stupid Car / You /
Thinking about You

Produced and engineered by the band's managers, Chris Hufford and Bryce Edge, *Drill* debuted on the UK charts at number 101. Hufford and Edge realized it was time to put someone else in the producer's seat. The versions of "You" and "Thinking about You" are the same as those on the *Manic Hedgehog* tape, while "Prove Yourself" differs from the version on *Pablo Honey*. All formats of the EP were limited to 3,000 copies. Expect to pay at least £60 (around US $120) for this collector's item.

Creep EP (21 September 1992)
CD / 12"/ cassette
Creep / Lurgee / Inside My Head /
Million $ Question

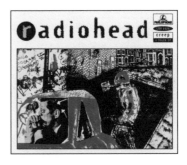

This was the first Radiohead release produced by Paul Kolderie and Sean Slade. The EP was originally intended to be a double-A-side single with "Inside My Head" and "Million $ Question," but after hearing "Creep" during a practice, Kolderie and Slade decided that it should be the A side. The release made it to number 78 on the UK singles chart and was played on Radio 1 only twice before being removed from rotation. All formats of the EP were limited to 6,000 copies.

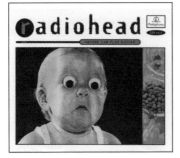

Anyone Can Play Guitar (1 February 1993)
CD / 12"/ cassette
Anyone Can Play Guitar / Faithless,
The Wonder Boy / Coke Babies

Released only a few weeks before *Pablo Honey*, this strong EP intensified people's interest in Radiohead. It reached number 32 on the UK charts and was named single of the week in *Melody Maker's* 23 January 1993 issue. This single, containing the only recorded version of "Coke Babies," has been deleted.

Pop Is Dead (10 May 1993)
CD / 12"/ cassette
Pop Is Dead / Banana Co.
(acoustic) / Creep (live) / Ripcord (live)

The first EP to be released with "Creep" as a B-side, but not the last. Sadly, Radiohead's other material was not attracting the fans they'd hoped it would, so the string of singles released at this time all contained versions of "Creep" as a sales booster. "Banana Co." is from a session on Signal Radio in Cheshire, and both "Creep" and "Ripcord" were recorded live at the band's Town and Country Club show in February 1993, at which they supported Belly. The record made it to number 42 on the UK singles chart. The number of copies pressed is unknown; this EP has long since been deleted.

Creep (reissue) (6 September 1993)
CD / Limited edition 7"/ cassette
Creep / Yes I Am / Blow Out (remix) / Inside My Head (live)
Limited edition 12"
Creep (acoustic) / You (live) / Vegetable (live) / Killer Cars (live)

The reissue of the EP wasn't the band's idea, but the success the single attained in America during the summer of 1993 created a demand in the UK for a rerelease of "Creep." The number embarked on a second life almost a year after its original release, debuting at number seven on the UK singles chart. The British EP is deleted and now goes for a hefty price. The single — with the same CD track listing — was released in Japan in June 1994 to coincide with Radiohead's first visit to that country. The 12" songs that were released became more readily available on another Japanese CD, entitled *Itch*.

My Iron Lung (26 September 1994)
CD1 and 12" (blue cover)
My Iron Lung / The Trickster /
Punchdrunk Lovesick Singalong /
Lozenge of Love

CD2 and 12" (red cover)
My Iron Lung / Lewis (Mistreated) /
Permanent Daylight / You Never Wash
Up after Yourself
Cassette
My Iron Lung / The Trickster / Lewis
(Mistreated) / Punchdrunk Lovesick
Singalong

This between-album EP reached number 24 on the singles charts and also represents Radiohead's move towards two-part singles. Variations of this EP were released around the world as different countries waited for new material from the band, though only in Australia was an EP released containing all six B-sides and "Creep" (acoustic), which is still available; the two British EPS, however, have been deleted.

High and Dry / Planet Telex
(17 February 1995)
CD1 (red cover)
High and Dry / Planet Telex / Maquiladora / Planet Telex (Hexadecimal Mix) [by Steve Osborne]

CD2 (blue cover)
High and Dry / Planet Telex / Killer Cars / Planet Telex (LFO Mix)
12"
Planet Telex (Hexadecimal Mix) [by Steve Osborne] / Planet Telex (LFO JD Mix) / Planet Telex (Hexadecimal Dub) [by Steve Osborne] / High and Dry
Promo 12" titled "Planet Telex: Club Mix DJ"
Planet Telex (Album Version) / Planet Telex (Hexadecimal Mix) [by Steve Osborne] / Planet Telex (LFO JD mix) [by LFO] / Planet Telex (Trashed Mix) [by Alien Beatfreak]

Radiohead still wasn't grabbing enough of the British market's attention. The second single before the release of *The Bends* debuted at number 17. The track listing for the Planet Telex: Club Mix DJ is as stated above, though some play the Hexadecimal Dub as the first track, along with two versions of the LFO mix. All of these EPS are rare, especially the Club Mix DJ 12".

Fake Plastic Trees (15 May 1995)
CD1 (blue cover) and cassette
Fake Plastic Trees / India Rubber / How Can You Be Sure?

CD2 (red cover)
Fake Plastic Trees / Fake Plastic Trees (acoustic) / Bullet Proof . . . I Wish I Was (acoustic) / Street Spirit (Fade Out) (acoustic)

This double EP, which features the first single to hit the North American market, fared worse than "High and Dry," entering the British singles charts at number 20. A special acoustic EP from a set Thom and Jonny performed at Eve's Club in London, CD2 came in a limited-edition pack with a poster depicting the band watching television. Both singles have been deleted.

Just (7 August 1995)
CD1 and cassette
Just / Planet Telex (Karma Sunra Mix) / Killer Cars (Mogadon Version)

CD2
Just / Bones (live) / Planet Telex (live) / Anyone Can Play Guitar (live)

"Just," the perfect rock song, with a mysterious video to accompany it, debuted on the British charts at number 19, making it seem as though Radiohead could never break into the top ten again, despite all the favorable reviews *The Bends* had won. The CD2 contains three live tracks from the band's performance at the Forum in London on 24 March 1995, packaged in a limited-edition box with two postcards of the band. Both singles have been deleted.

Help! EP (16 October 1995)
CD and cassette
Lucky

Possibly one of the greatest disappointments in recent British music history: this single was released just after Radio 1 brass had decided they'd promoted enough charity records; "Lucky" was ignored as a radio single, thus hurting the EP release. The song debuted at number 51 before falling off the charts. This was a huge letdown because proceeds from the single were earmarked for the War Child Fund — and because the lead-off song was one the band truly loved.

Street Spirit (Fade Out) (22 January 1996)
CD1 (escalator cover)
Street Spirit (Fade Out) / Talk Show Host / Bishop's Robes

CD2 *(cat cover)*
Street Spirit (Fade Out) / Banana Co. / Molasses
7"
Street Spirit (Fade Out) / Bishop's Robes

After the press had credited Radiohead with having created one of the best albums of the year, EMI cagily held back this single from the Christmas competition and released it soon after New Year's, while *The Bends* was still fresh in everyone's mind. The result: it debuted at number five. And *The Bends* hit a new high point during the same week, attaining number four.

Paranoid Android (26 May 1997)
CD1 (white cover)
Paranoid Android / Polyethelene (Parts 1 & 2) / Pearly*

CD2 (purple cover)
Paranoid Android / A Reminder / Melatonin
7" (clear blue)
Paranoid Android / Polyethelene (Parts 1 & 2)

A true return to form, this double EP was Radiohead's best-ever showing on the UK singles charts, selling 94,000 copies in one week and reaching number three. Unfortunately, Hanson's "Mmmbop" was released in the UK the same week, pushing the number-one spot beyond Radiohead's grasp.

Karma Police (25 August 1997)
CD1 (white cover)
Karma Police / Meeting in the Aisle / Lull

CD2 (blue cover)
Karma Police / Climbing up the Walls
(Zero 7 Mix) / Climbing up the Walls (Fila
Brazillia Mix)
12"
Karma Police / Meeting in the Aisle /
Climbing up the Walls (Zero 7 Mix)

Released in the UK as the band was finishing up its summer tour in the United States, this double EP debuted at number eight. The single fell off the charts quickly, but the accompanying Hitchcockian video remained in rotation on video stations for quite some time.

No Surprises (12 January 1998)
CD1 (white cover) and cassette
No Surprises / Palo Alto / How I Made
My Millions

CD2 (YELLOW COVER) No Surprises / Airbag
(live) / Lucky (live)
12"
No Surprises / Palo Alto

This double EP was in a position similar to that of "Street Spirit" in 1996. It came out right after all of the year's-best-list compilers had declared *OK Computer* the greatest album of the year. Facing stiff competition from Oasis's long-awaited "All around the World," "No Surprises" couldn't gain the upper hand but did reach number four on the UK singles charts.

Creep (June 1993)
Creep / The Bends (live) / Prove Yourself (live) / Creep (live)

This France-only single was the first release to contain "The Bends," which dates the song long before its official studio release. The tracks were taped live for *The Black Session*, a French radio show on which bands preview their forthcoming releases. Radiohead's session was on 23 February 1993.

Creep (1993)
Creep / Yes I Am / Inside My Head (live) / Creep (acoustic)

While not readily available, this CD single is still easier to track down and cheaper than all the other "Creep" EPs. It was released in the Netherlands.

Stop Whispering (October 1993)
Stop Whispering (US Version) / Creep (acoustic) / Pop Is Dead / Inside My Head (live)

Released as a single in the United States, this track climbed the *Billboard Modern Rock* charts to number 24 but immediately fell off.

Itch (June 1994)
Stop Whispering (US Version) / Thinking about You (*Drill* EP Version) / Faithless, The Wonder Boy / Banana Co. (acoustic) / Killer Cars (live) / Vegetable (live) / You (live) / Creep (acoustic)

This Japanese-only release contained only previously released material, but some of the songs are very hard to come by ("Killer Cars," "You," and "Vegetable" are only available on the "Creep" reissue 12"). An expensive release, it is not difficult to track down and has not been deleted. The EP was released in Japan in 1994; EMI Japan wanted to offer fans a little sustenance as they eagerly awaited *The Bends*.

High and Dry Live Package (1995)
High and Dry / Creep (live) / My Iron Lung (live) / Stop Whispering (live) / Punchdrunk Lovesick Singalong (live)

Still fairly easy to track down, though somewhat expensive, this EP was released in the Netherlands and contains four live tracks recorded at the Melkweg in Amsterdam on 2 December 1994. The final track on the EP, "Punchdrunk Lovesick Singalong," is a rarity in the band's live set, and therefore a must for collectors.

The Bends (1996)
The Bends / My Iron Lung (live) / Bones (live)

This is a special Irish-only release that features "The Bends" as lead-off single. Beware: many copies of this single contain "Planet Telex" instead — a record-company error. The two live songs, the same on all releases, were recorded at the Forum in London on 24 March 1995. The cover, appropriately enough, depicts an inhaler.

Live EP (also called **Pinkpop Single**) (1996)
Fake Plastic Trees (live) / Blow Out (live) / Bones (live) / You (live) / High and Dry (live)

Released in the Netherlands to coincide with the band's headlining performance at the Pinkpop Festival in the summer of 1996, this EP is an exceptionally high-quality recording of a Radiohead gig at Rock City in Nottingham, England, on 5 November 1995. Some CDS have "Nice Dream" instead of "You" as track four, but the track listing for all releases says "You."

No Surprises / Running from Demons
(10 December 1997)
No Surprises / Pearly* (remix) / Melatonin / Meeting in the Aisle / Bishop's Robes / A Reminder

167

A special Japan-only release (the packaging states clearly that it is "a mini-album aimed at the Japanese Market"), this EP contains an exclusive remix of "Pearly*." It was released to coincide with Radiohead's January 1998 tour of Japan.

Airbag/How's My Driving? (21 April 1998)
Airbag / Melatonin / Pearly* / A Reminder / Polyethylene (Pts. 1 & 2) / Palo Alto / Meeting in the Aisle

A special release for North America, this compiles B-sides from a few of the *OK Computer* singles. The EP entered the *Billboard* Top 200 Albums chart at number 56, Radiohead's second-best debut on the US chart. It quickly fell off, but given that the EP was released around the time Radiohead's sold-out 1998 tour was in progress, it shows that there was a buzz going around. The EP was nominated for Best Alternative Music Performance for the 1999 Grammy Awards.

Albums

Pablo Honey (22 February 1993 [UK]; 20 April 1993 [US])
You / Creep / How Do You? / Thinking about You / Stop Whispering / Anyone Can Play Guitar / Ripcord / Vegetable / Prove Yourself / Lurgee / I Can't / Blow Out

Pablo Honey debuted on the UK charts at number 25, and while it has never surpassed this position, it has returned to the top 40 over the following years as Radiohead's success has grown. In the United States, it slowly climbed the charts after getting off to a very slow start. By 7 August it was at number 32, where it remained for the next four weeks before dropping to number 33, where it stayed for two more weeks, and then dropped out of the top 40 altogether. It held a spot on *Billboard'*s Top 200 Albums chart for six months.

The North American release of the album included the radio edit of "Creep" as a thirteenth track. The Japanese version included five extra tracks — "Inside My Head," "Million $ Question," "Pop Is Dead," "Creep" (live), and "Ripcord" (live) — which were the B-sides from the original "Creep" single and the songs from the "Pop Is Dead" single minus "Banana Co." (acoustic).

The Bends (13 March 1995 [UK];
4 April 1995 [US];
28 March 1995 [Canada];
16 March 1995 [Japan])
Planet Telex / The Bends / High and Dry
/ Fake Plastic Trees / Bones / (Nice
Dream) / Just / My Iron Lung / Bullet
Proof . . . I Wish I Was / Black Star / Sulk
/ Street Spirit (Fade Out)

In the UK, *The Bends* debuted at number six, but
it wasn't able to hold on for very long. The album was a slow burner and didn't
leave the charts or vanish from the public eye for many months. It peaked at number four in January of 1996 after the year-end critics' polls had all screamed its
praises, and during the same week "Street Spirit" was released as a single.

In the US, *The Bends* didn't have the support of a hit single the way *Pablo Honey*
had, and so it debuted at number 88. Over time, *The Bends* outsold *Pablo Honey*
in every single country except for the US.

As with *Pablo Honey*, pressings of *The Bends* in other countries included bonus
tracks or, in some cases, a second CD. The Japanese version came with two extra
tracks: "How Can You Be Sure?" (titled "When I'm Like This" on the original
pressing) and "Killer Cars." In France, limited-edition copies of the album came
with a free live CD, either *Live au Forum* (which contained "Just", "Bones" (live),
"Planet Telex" (live), and "Anyone Can Play Guitar" (live); the live tracks were
taken from the band's show at the Forum on 24 March 1995) or *Live à l' Astoria*
(which contained the tracks "My Iron Lung" (live), "Just" (live), and
"Maquiladora" (live), recorded at the Astoria on 27 May 1994). In the
Netherlands, some copies of the album were released with the *Pinkpop Single*.

Phil: "The Bends *was like* Star Wars — *a neat, separate entity with
lots of explosions but not much plot. And* OK Computer *is* The Empire
Strikes Back — *more ambitious, more complex, with more loose
ends, but ultimately much better. Our next album won' t be* Return of
the Jedi *though, because that was rubbish."*

Colin: "And Pablo Honey *was actually something like* Battlestar
Gallactica. *A low budget, poor quality version of the real thing"*
(*Sutherland, "Rounding the Bends"*).

OK Computer (16 June 1997 [UK];
17 June 1997 [Canada];
1 July 1997 [US])
Airbag / Paranoid Android / Subterranean
Homesick Alien / Exit Music (For a Film) /
Let Down / Karma Police / Fitter Happier /
Electioneering / Climbing up the Walls / No
Surprises / Lucky / The Tourist

This album debuted at number one in the UK, and at the end of the year was on the top-five lists of over a hundred magazines worldwide (in fact, it was among the top three on over half these magazine lists). This is by far the band's best-selling album in every country it was released in. It landed at number eight on the UK's list of top-ten-best-selling albums of 1997. In the United States, it debuted at number 21 on the *Billboard* charts and, after a year, went platinum.

One special release came out in the Netherlands: it included a second CD featuring "Karma Police" with the B-sides "A Reminder" and "Melatonin." This double-CD set was limited to 40,000 copies. It includes a special sticker with the image of two figures, one with a briefcase, shaking hands.

Compilations

Volume 7 (July 1993)
Stupid Car (Tinnitus Mix)

Volume is a popular booklet that includes CDs filled with rare tracks from different artists in the indie world. These CDs rarely incorporate album tracks, and feature debut releases from two or three new acts per issue. The booklets are almost two hundred pages long and contain intriguing interviews with the artists on CD. This particular issue features a mix of "Stupid Car," which is otherwise available only in its original form, on the *Drill* EP. The *Volume* series issued a best of *Volume* release in June of 1995 entitled *Sharks Patrol These Waters*, a two-CD set that also includes this Radiohead rarity.

Criminal Justice! Axe the Act (July 1995)
Banana Co.

A special benefit release (proceeds went to the Coalition Against the Criminal Justice Act) featuring a wide range of music, this CD includes the studio recording of "Banana Co." done with John Leckie in 1994. This version later appeared as a B-side to the "Street Spirit (Fade Out)" single.

Clueless Soundtrack (18 July 1995)
Fake Plastic Trees (acoustic)

This soundtrack contains the same acoustic version of the track that appears on the *Fake Plastic Trees* CD2 in the single set, but since the EP has long since been deleted, this may be your only available source for a sparse, lovely version of a wonderful "complaint rock" track.

... Hold On: BBC Radio 1 FM Sessions (1995)
Street Spirit (live)

This benefit compilation is filled with Radio 1 performances by bands such as Suede, Teenage Fanclub, Drugstore, and Grant Lee Buffalo. Radiohead's performance comes from a 14 September 1994 evening session. Proceeds went to the Samaritans, a charity that funds a confidential support line for people in crisis.

Volume 13 (February 1995)
Nice Dream (demo)

Many bands were featured in the *Volume* series more than once, including Radiohead. This issue also contains exclusive tracks by Elcka, Throwing Muses, and the Boo Radleys. Radiohead's contribution, "Nice Dream," is an interesting variation with different lyrics to the second verse. The albums in the *Volume* series are limited editions, so this one may be difficult to come by — but it's well worth the search.

2 Meter Sessies: Volume 6 (December 1995)
My Iron Lung (live)

The *2 Meter Sessies* (Dutch for "sessions") is a Netherlands radio program featuring live performances by bands from all over the world, and from these performances various compilations have been created. Radiohead attended the sessions on 22 February 1995 at Bullet Sound Studios, and their stunning performance of "My Iron Lung" was placed in the sixth volume of the CD series. Here the chorus is clear and comprehensible.

Help! (9 September 1995 [UK]; 17 October 1995 [US])
Lucky

Help! was a benefit release created by Tony Crean, Terri Hall, and Anton Brookes. Several different bands headed into the studios on 4 September and recorded their songs, which were produced and mastered over the next two days so the album could hit UK shops by the weekend — 9 September. "Lucky" is debuted on this release, and while the band tried to work out a different version for *OK Computer*, they soon realized they didn't want to change this utterly perfect song. The proceeds from this release went to the War Child Fund, an organization that, among other things, sent food, clothing, and medical supplies to children in Croatia and Bosnia.

Rock the Vote (1996)
Planet Telex (Hexadecimal Mix)

This was a special British-only compilation released to encourage young people to get out and vote during England's general election. It's the same version of "Planet Telex" as the one on the *High and Dry/Planet Telex* CD1.

Evening Session Priority Tunes (December 1996)
Just (session) / Street Spirit

The title of this British-only two-CD set is deceiving because of its 41 tracks only nine were actually taped from the *Evening Session*; the other songs had been previously released. Of the two Radiohead tracks featured, "Just" is the only live recording, taped during the band's 14 September 1994 session.

Later Volume One: Brit Beat (September 1996)
The Bends (live)

This British CD was supposed to be the first of a series documenting performances from the TV show *Later with Jools Holland*. An intriguing performance of this live favorite, the track stands out clearly as one of the best on the compilation.

Just Passin' Through (1996)
Street Spirit (acoustic)

A special benefit CD for Health Care for the Homeless, Inc. that was released by radio station WHFS-FM in the US, this release features a beautiful solo acoustic version of "Street Spirit (Fade Out)" that Thom performed live at the station in Rockville, Maryland, on 21 April 1996.

Romeo and Juliet Soundtrack Vol. 1 (29 October 1996)
Talk Show Host (Nellee Hooper Mix)

An excellent version of the song that originated as a "Street Spirit (Fade Out)" B-side, this mix is less guitar-oriented and has more beats and electronic sounds humming throughout. The success of the soundtrack — and the fact that this is an amazing song — led to the number being included in the band's live set during the *OK Computer* tour.

Altered States (November 1996)
Planet Telex (Depthcharge Mix)

A wonderful two-CD compilation featuring tracks by popular bands that have been remixed into dance versions. This is a British-only release, so it's difficult to find, but it would make a worthy addition to any collection of Radiohead rarities. The track is available exclusively on *Altered States*.

Foundations: Coming up from the Streets (20 January 1997)
Talk Show Host (Black Dog Remix)

Yet another British-only compilation of ambient or drum 'n' bass tracks. This version of "Talk Show Host," remixed by Black Dog and Webby, is by far the most unusual. Again, this compilation is the only source for this particular version of the song. Proceeds from the release were earmarked for the Big Issue Foundation, which has set up various initiatives to help out homeless people throughout the UK.

Music from the Gregg Araki Movie *Nowhere* (25 March 1997)
How Can You Be Sure?

Used in the film *Nowhere*, "How Can You Be Sure?" was a radio single in Canada and did well in the period leading up to the release of *OK Computer*. This version is identical to the one on *Fake Plastic Trees* CD1, but since the CD, like many Radiohead releases, was deleted some time ago, the soundtrack may represent your easiest (and cheapest) access to the track.

Het Beste Uit 10 Jaar *2 Meter Sessies* (1997)
Fake Plastic Trees (live)

This Netherlands-only double CD (with a title that translates loosely as "The Best of the *2 Meter Sessions*" features a wide array of artists and is definitely worth hunting down. It has Radiohead performing "Fake Plastic Trees" at the session they attended on 22 February 1995 at Bullet Sound Studios. This performance is truly unique in that the vocals are brought to the foreground of the recording — it sounds quite different from other live recordings. The CD-ROM material includes a picture of Jonny in action and the band's set list for their performance.

Romeo and Juliet **Soundtrack Vol. 2** (8 April 1997)
Introduction of Romeo / Mantua

The second volume of this soundtrack does not contain any Radiohead tracks, though it had been rumored for the longest time that "Exit Music (For a Film)" would be included. Here, instead, is mainly instrumental music used as background in the movie as well as some of the actors' dialogue. The two listed tracks utilize portions of the Nellee Hooper mixes of "Talk Show Host."

Long Live Tibet
The Bends (demo)

This British-only album featuring various UK acts was made to raise money for the Tibet House Trust, a charity for the people of Tibet. Included is a very early version of "The Bends" with heavy guitar and slightly different lyrics.

Glastonbury Live 97: Mud for It (August 1997)
Paranoid Android (live)

This special release features one track each from several artists who performed at Glastonbury in 1997. It is the only "official" taste of this monumental performance available.

Launch CD-ROM Issue No. 15. (October 1997)
Audio
Lucky (live)
CD-ROM *video*
Interview with Thom and Jonny / Lucky (live)

Not really a compilation, this release is actually a CD-ROM magazine that features Radiohead as its cover story. It comes with an exclusive version of Radiohead performing "Lucky" in Washington with no audience. You can play this track on a CD player or watch the performance on the CD-ROM. The CD-ROM also has an interview segment that shows Thom and Jonny sitting down and displays a list of topics between them. When you click on a topic, the two come alive and begin answering the questions. An item to treasure.

Tibetan Freedom Concert (4 November 1997)
Fake Plastic Trees (live)

A triple-CD pack that features various artists who appeared at the 1997 concert (and a couple from the 1996 show). Radiohead's contribution is an amazing, full-band version of this live favorite. The Milarepa Fund, which spreads the word about the problems facing the people of Tibet, was awarded the money this project raised.

MTV 120 Minutes Live (3 February 1998)
Fake Plastic Trees (live)

The liner notes of this compilation state that Radiohead's offering should "definitely be the closing track," and when you hear the passion and intensity in Thom's voice you'll know why.

CMJ CD Sampler Vol. 56 (March 1998)
No Surprises (live)

This CD is only available with the April 1998 issue of the *College Music Journal*. It contains a live version of "No Surprises" taken from Radiohead's infamous televised Hammerstein Ballroom show, which took place on 19 December 1997 in New York City.

Blowout (March 1998)
Planet Telex (Hexadecimal Dub)

This compilation is filled with previously recorded material, but the Radiohead track is a rarity simply because it is otherwise available solely on the *High and Dry* 12". It is, therefore, the only CD version.

Rare on the Air 4 (6 October 1998)
Subterranean Homesick Alien (acoustic)

This compilation allows those without access to bootlegs to hear the early versions of *OK Computer* songs. It documents the first time "Subterranean Homesick Alien" was ever played on radio: on 4 April 1995 for *Morning becomes Eclectic* on Santa Monica's KCRW 89.9 (the CD gives a different date, but this performance actually took place the day *The Bends* was released in the US). In this acoustic version, both verses are sung together and then the chorus closes the song. Definitely a worthwhile addition to any collection.

Videos

Live at the Astoria (March 1995)
You / Bones / Ripcord / Black Star / Creep / The Bends / My Iron Lung / Prove Yourself / Maquiladora / Vegetable / Fake Plastic Trees / Just / Stop Whispering / Anyone Can Play Guitar / Street Spirit (Fade Out) / Pop Is Dead / Blow Out

A special video of the Radiohead London Astoria gig on 27 May 1994. This show was an intriguing one: the band played a number of songs from *The Bends* that would not be released until ten months later. The video was released in Britain only, and is a very expensive import (due to the different video format).

Seven Television Commercials (30 June 1998)
Paranoid Android / Street Spirit / No Surprises / Just / High and Dry (US Version) / Karma Police / Fake Plastic Trees

This video compilation, wrapped in polyethylene and released in mid-1998, contains clips of songs from both *The Bends* and *OK Computer*. Because certain video stations felt the need to edit "Paranoid Android," watching this compilation may be your only sure way to see the unadulterated version.

Meeting People Is Easy (16 November 1998 [UK])

This Grant Gee video creation documents a Radiohead tour throughout 1997 and into the early part of 1998. Included are segments from the band's performances during a promotional circus in Barcelona, some footage shot in Paris, clips from a special MTV show held at New York's Hammerstein Ballroom in December of 1997, and footage of band members and journalists reacting to them in Tokyo. The video is, essentially, an honest look at Radiohead's busy life during this time. Incorporating a few clips of new songs, it also provides fans with a taste of things to come.

Collaborations

Come Again (September 1997)
Sparklehorse with Thom Yorke, Wish You Were Here

A universally slagged compilation of (mostly) terrible cover songs by contemporary bands. If you are not interested in Sparklehorse, don't waste your money (Thom's role, as mentioned in the songbook, is *very* small). This is a double-album British-only release, and it's very expensive. If you really need to have the song, pick up Sparklehorse's double-A-side British single "Painbirds / Maria's Little Elbows," where it appears as a B-side.

White Magic for Lovers (5 May 1998 [UK]; 8 June 1998 [US])
Drugstore with Thom Yorke, El President

"El President" was the first single from Drugstore's wonderfully diverse second album. The song was also released as a two-part CD single and debuted at number 20 on the singles charts before diving off them.

Psyence Fiction (24 August 1998 [UK]; 29 September 1998 [US])
DJ Shadow with Thom Yorke, Rabbit in Your Headlights

This collaboration was easily the most anticipated of the year. The album entered the British charts at number one, both because of Thom's contribution and because it was the first new work from DJ Shadow in some time. While many fans may just want to hear the Yorke-Shadow collaboration, this brilliant album is well worth owning.

175

Velvet Goldmine Soundtrack (28 September 1998)

Venus in Furs (featuring Jonny on guitar and Thom on guitar and vocals), 2HB / Ladytron / Baby's on Fire / Bitter-Sweet / Tumbling Down

A compendium of original glam-rock creations from the early 1970s and a few covers of early classics by contemporary acts. Thom and Jonny help out as part of the band Venus in Furs, which does three Roxy Music songs (with Thom singing); they also play guitar on "Baby's on Fire" and "Tumbling Down" while Jonathan Rhys Meyers provides vocals. Despite the fact that the album received mixed reviews, these covers are truly intriguing.

Rabbit in Your Headlights (12 October 1998)

DJ Shadow with Thom Yorke, Rabbit in Your Headlights / Rabbit in Your Headlights (Instrumental) / Rabbit in Your Headlights (Underdog Mix) / Rabbit in Your Headlights (Underdog Instrumental) / Rabbit in Your Headlights (3D Mix [Reverse Light]) / Rabbit in Your Headlights (3D Mix [Reverse Light Instrumental]) / Rabbit in Your Headlights (David Axelrod, Suburban Hell Mix)

There was great anticipation for this EP but it never entered the British charts; because it has more than two B-sides, it was ruled ineligible and could not be ranked. Regardless, this is a brilliant EP. Unlike many of the "Planet Telex" remixes, these new versions of "Rabbit in Your Headlights" are wildly different from the original and just as interesting. Accompanying the single was a very disturbing video created by Jonathan Glazer, which depicts a man, who has taken the place of a rabbit, walking down a street in a tunnel; he is continually hit by callous drivers who then speed on. Only one car slows down, but the man, who screams and yells to himself while walking, is too overwhelmed by his own anger to pay attention to the driver. Miraculously, and with the aid of some unbelievable camera techniques, the final car that tries to knock the man aside explodes on impact. The visuals are as moving as the song.

influences,
collaborators,
and colleagues

These bands and individual artists have all, in some way, played a role in shaping Radiohead's history. This is a short list of all those who have collaborated with Thom and/or Jonny, as well as those who have paid tribute to the band. I haven't cited every single one of the hundreds of acts that have had an impact on Radiohead though I have mentioned a couple. I've also included one related act.

Elvis Costello

Elvis Costello has influenced hundreds of budding musicians, Thom among them. Costello has an elegant way of combining clever, moving lyrics with various styles of music; the results are powerful and intelligent. Thom first got into Costello in 1986 when he heard "I'll Wear It Proudly" from the album *King of America*. He realized he'd found someone who felt the way he did, and who knew how to write about it directly. Costello's example gave Thom the confidence to write his own songs in a very serious, personal way without becoming totally self-absorbed and shutting out the audience.

Thom has identified Costello's *Blood and Chocolate*, released the same year, as one of his favorites by the artist. The album contains "Tokyo Storm Warning," which Thom considered wondrous gibberish — everything a song should be. Thom's interest in Costello impacted On a Friday's roster. That early incarnation of Radiohead often played "Pump It Up" from Costello's 1978 album *This Year's Model*.

In mid-1995, Thom met Costello when the band did the TV show *Later with Jools Holland*. That night Thom was ecstatic; the meeting meant so much to him that he dreamt about it for the next six months. At the end of 1997, Costello cited *OK Computer* as one of his favorite releases of the year.

Costello has said, "Thom Yorke's mentioned my name a few times. Of the people who are around at the moment you couldn't have anyone more talented than him paying you a compliment. *OK Computer* was one of the great records of the year. In the kind of music that I do, which I suppose is songs, and how you then explode them out, they're doing it as boldly as anybody" (Du Noyer).

REM

When REM hit the music scene back in the early 1980s, their music was deemed innovative and unusual. Their following grew throughout the decade until they, the Smiths, and U2 were considered the most influential acts of the decade. The On a Friday boys became fans of REM's work early on, finding inspiration both in the lyrics (including the fact that the words were difficult to make out) and the innovative music.

In July 1995, Radiohead had the great honor of opening for REM during part of that band's European *Monster* tour, and then for a month in the United States. The members of the two bands became good friends, and Radiohead learned a great deal from REM about surviving in the music industry. "What REM gave us was a sense that you can be as emotional as you like in what you do," explains Thom. "That's what it's about. It was extraordinarily good therapy" (Brown).

Michael Stipe, REM's lead singer, became a huge fan of Radiohead over the course of the tour and continued to follow the band throughout their *OK Computer* shows. He also brought Thom and Jonny into the *Velvet Goldmine* soundtrack project, for which the pair played in a band called Venus in Furs and performed Roxy Music covers.

Can

Many of the articles on *The Bends* or *OK Computer* mention the influence of Can's album *Tago Mago*, a personal favorite of both Thom and Jonny. This innovative 1970s band made very difficult — even inaccessible — experimental music, pioneering with synthesizers, early electronic styles, and the concept of cutting and pasting parts of songs.

Can recorded their albums wherever they pleased and maintained complete control, an ideology that Radiohead adopted when it came time to record *OK Computer*. Although Can is not an easy listen for many, the band's influence on contemporary music is immeasurable.

Lunatic Calm (formerly Flicker Noise)

Lunatic Calm is fronted by sHack. With Thom, sHack started the Exeter band Headless Chicken, which soon became just Headless. After Thom left for Oxford, decapitating Headless, sHack started Flicker Noise, for which he was programmer and vocalist (Thom returned to Exeter to play guitar with the band, but only played one gig before making a full-time commitment to On a Friday). Flicker Noise released a debut single, "Information Is Power," along with a few other records, before becoming Lunatic Calm, which has found success in North America. Their debut album, *Metropol*, is an intense industrial/techno experience that encapsulates many of the ideas found in Nine Inch Nails's work, but takes the listener on a much more interesting journey.

Drugstore

Drugstore formed in 1992, and despite its slow beginning, built a following within a couple of years. Band members became friends with the Radiohead boys in mid-1994, and in 1995 the two acts toured North American clubs, Radiohead supporting *The Bends* and Drugstore their self-titled debut album. Later in the year, they played a few dates in Europe together, winding up at the Luna Theatre in Belgium on 5 December 1995. Driving in from Holland the day before, Drugstore's lead singer, Isabel Monteiro, wrote a special song. Introducing "My Radiohead," she said: "I thought, we've got to come up with something for Radiohead because they have been so cool and so nice to us, not only the band but the crew as well. I thought, what can I give them? I offered them my body, they turned me down. I offered them the drummer, they wouldn't want him. I offered them my guitar player, and they said, 'No.' So we thought, 'Fuck it, we're gonna write Radiohead a little song called My Radiohead.'" The lyrics mention every member of Radiohead and include a few Radiohead song titles.

In 1996, Drugstore began covering "Black Star" in their set, and have done so periodically ever since. Also in that year, Monteiro wrote a song she felt would sound perfect with Thom helping with the vocals. It was titled "El President," but due to problems that Drugstore's label, Go! Discs, was having, the song was not officially released until 1998, when it became the lead-off single on Drugstore's sophomore release, *White Magic for Lovers*. During the live sets the band played while promoting the album, Thom never joined them, though Isabel often said that he was with her in spirit.

Sparklehorse

In 1995, Radiohead toured with the innovative, country-rock-influenced band Sparklehorse. The Oxford quintet was blown away by this American act. Jonny later admitted that Sparklehorse's musical style, which at the time could be heard on the band's album *Vivadixiesubmarinetransimissionplot*, was one of the styles Radiohead tried to emulate in the studio while making *OK Computer*. In 1997, Sparklehorse recorded Pink Floyd's "Wish You Were Here" with Thom phoning in backing vocals and television sounds.

Sparklehorse lead singer Mark Linkous says of Yorke: "His lyrics are so beautiful and genuinely . . . I don't even know the word for it. But that's all part of life: some of it's disturbing. And it takes a lot to try to find the pretty things in the ugliness. You know, I think a lot of people think Thom is ugly. You know, his eye is kinda odd, and his face can look a bit scrunched up. It's weird. Our favorite part of the human body is the eyes, because you can see through them what's in the person, and even in the one eye you can see of Thom's, you can tell he's beautiful" (Nine, "Spiders").

DJ Shadow

Shadow, whose real name is Josh Davis, is a unique artist whose love of hip hop and sampling comes together on his EPs and his debut album, *Endtruducing*. While DJ Shadow's music is largely instrumental, his tempo, hypnotic beats, and eclectic samples have left many believing that he is one of the music world's front-runners. The members of Radiohead all love his music passionately. Says Ed: "As with a lot of the Mo' Wax stuff he isn't so much about writing a song as such as creating this brilliant world of ebb and flow, and depth and texture" ("100 Most Important"). Shadow's work has influenced many artists. Radiohead has identified him as the inspiration for "Airbag" and "Paranoid Android." The respect is mutual.

James Lavelle, head of the Mo' Wax label, which DJ Shadow records for, says of Radiohead: "I really liked their work on *The Bends* and the emotions in the songs and sounds. I told [Shadow] to check their stuff out. Originally I was going to collaborate with the band as a whole but I think [Thom] wanted to step away from what he was doing[,] it was an opportunity for him to do something completely different" (Burgess).

This collaboration was the UNKLE project for which DJ Shadow and Thom teamed up to make "Rabbit in Your Headlights." The track was so strong that it became the lead-off single on the UNKLE album *Psyence Fiction*.

Massive Attack

An exceptional band from Bristol, England, that moved to the forefront of the trip-hop scene, Massive Attack has continued to release wonderful albums while becoming well-known for its cutting-edge remixes. In 1997, the band joined up with Radiohead to play the Royal Dublin Showgrounds before an audience of over 35,000. After *OK Computer* was released, Massive Attack and Radiohead began talking. They were considering the idea of Massive Attack completely remixing the entire album. But Massive Attack was still hard at work on the album *Mezzanine*, and so the idea was shelved for the rest of 1997. There's still talk of Massive Attack remixing some Radiohead tracks when schedules allow.

Massive Attack member Robert Del Naja (aka 3D) did remix Thom's collaboration with DJ Shadow, "Rabbit in Your Headlights," doing both an alluring reverse light mix and an instrumental mix.

Bernard Butler

In 1992 Bernard Butler hit the music scene as the brash, talented guitarist for the glam-rock outfit Suede. His talents defined the band's releases up until 1994, when the masterpiece *Dog Man Star* came out; at this time Butler decided to leave the group due to differences of opinion he was having with other band members. Shortly after that, he collaborated with David McAlmont on a string of singles, but then they, too, parted ways. Still, many music fans who heard Butler's stellar playing, including Jonny, became instant fans of his style. It was thus a great honor for Jonny to play with Butler when the two, along with Thom, became a part of the band Venus in Furs for the *Velvet Goldmine* soundtrack, put together by Michael Stipe.

Of the recording sessions with Jonny, Butler says: "Jonny was amazing. I'd never played with another guitar player before, but it worked really well. I'm a big fan of his and it turned out he really liked my stuff as well" (Wilkinson). Butler has been a fan of Radiohead's for years. At the end of 1995, he sang the praises of *The Bends*, calling it a "beautiful, nasty, down, high, confused [album] — very mid-nineties. Too modern to be fashionable, and hopefully they'll stay that way" ("Best Thing").

Spirit of the West

Spirit of the West is a popular, Celtic-tinged Canadian band that emerged in the mid-1980s. The group is fronted by singer/songwriters John Mann and Geoffrey Kelly. On their album *Open Heart Symphony* is a tribute song for Thom Yorke. The song, "Let the Ass Bray," was inspired by Radiohead's acoustic performance at Vancouver's Railway Club on 30 March 1995, in which Thom and Jonny were promoting *The Bends*. A young woman in the audience kept crying out for "Creep." Geoffrey Kelly told me that the two, tired out from touring, and Thom, in particular, suffering from the effects air travel was having on his ears, "got really fed up." Thom advised the girl to "Fuck off." What Thom didn't take into account, however, was that the venue was to many people like a home away from home. "It was like telling someone to fuck off in their own living room," says Kelly. "People started booing and hissing and Thom Yorke called them the rudest audience he'd ever seen."

Instead of lashing out at the British singer, Mann wrote a song that expresses both his outrage and his respect. He sings, "I wanted to hate you / Until I heard your voice." Spirit of the West members like to write brief descriptions or dedications for their songs and include them in their album booklets. For "Let the Ass Bray," Mann wrote: "Dear Thom of Radiohead, Some things are better left unsaid."

Gorky's Zygotic Mynci

One of the many bands to rise within the burgeoning Welsh music scene, Gorky's Zygotic Mynci is known for its unique, experimental, art-rock sound. The only connection between this band and Radiohead exists in Gorky's video for their song "Sweet Johnny," released in the summer of 1998. The video features puppets reen-acting other popular rock videos, such as the clip for the Verve's "Bittersweet Symphony" — a puppet mimicking Richard Ashcroft walks down a street. We also see a puppet submerged in water as in the video for "No Surprises."

Credit to the Nation

Not a band normally associated with Radiohead, this British hip-hop act released a single in August 1998 called "Tacky Love Song." The main sample in the song is the guitar riff from "High and Dry." Although they are immersed in England's hip-hop and under-ground grooves, Credit to the Nation obviously love the music of the Oxford fivesome. As for the song itself, it will most likely make you grab for *The Bends* before it's even finished — you'll want to hear the real thing.

Unbelievable Truth

Unbelievable Truth is a unique acoustic trio with an excellent sound and brilliant songs: the group deserves our full attention for this alone. But the lead singer of the band is Andy Yorke, Thom's brother. Although Unbelievable Truth must live in the shadow of Thom's more popular act, its debut album, *Almost Here*, or any of its EPS, prove that this project is in no way a Radiohead rip-off. Track down a copy of the *Stone* EP, listen to "Roadside No. 1," and feel your heart melt as the piano picks up midway through the track. Perhaps, in some cases, musical talent is genetic.

Other Influential or Favorite Releases

Over the years, Radiohead members have cited a range of albums as sources of inspiration. Aside from the releases of the acts I've just talked about, the following should be added to the list of Radiohead influences or personal favorites: Miles Davis, *Bitches Brew*; Laika, *Sounds of Satellites*; Joy Division, *Unknown Pleasures* and *Atmosphere*;

Tim Buckley, *Happy Sad*; Magazine, *Real Life*; Teenage Fanclub, *Songs from Northern Britain*; Buffalo Tom, *Let Me Come Over*; Lee "Scratch" Perry, *Arkology*; Björk, *Post* and *Homogenic*; Nick Drake, *Five Leaves Left*; Marvin Gaye, *What's Going On*; The Beach Boys, *Pet Sounds*; Various Artists, *Headz*; Spiritualized, *Ladies and Gentlemen We Are Floating in Space*; the works of Penderecki and film-score composer Ennio Morricone.

works consulted

Adams, Cameron. "Is Radiohead the New Pink Floyd?" *Rolling Stone Australia* Oct. 1997.

Arthur, Richard, et al. "Radiohead Discography Part 1: Official Releases." *Planet Telex*. 5 June 1998.
http://www.underworld.net/radiohead/discography/radio-1.txt

Atwood, Brett. "Radiohead Clip 'Just' Lies Down." *Billboard* 21 Oct. 1995.

———. "Radiohead Creeps Past Early Success." *Billboard* 25 Feb. 1995.

Bailie, Stuart. "Go Wired in the Country." *New Musical Express* 28 June 1997.

———. "Viva la Megabytes." *New Musical Express* 21 June 1997.

Baily, Kathryn. "Radiohead: Putting Creep to Sleep." *Chart* Aug. 1995.

Baimbridge, Richard. "Creep Show." *Dallas Observer* 24 July 1997.

Baker, Mike. "Radiohead: Three Way Jam." *Guitar Player* July 1996.

Barringer, Holly. "All You Need Is Loathe." *Melody Maker* 11 June 1994.

Barzillo, Carrie. "MTV Modern Rock Keys to Success for Capital Bands." *Billboard* 28 Aug. 1993.

Berketo, Steve. "Radio Head." *Extreme* July/Aug. 1995.

"The Best Thing I've Heard All Year." *Mojo* Jan. 1996.

Blashill, Pat. "The Year in Music: Band of the Year." *Spin* Jan. 1998.

Bondi, Kim. "The Radiohead Listening Hour." *No Frills* 1995.

Bowcott, Nick, et al. "Readers Choice: 100 Greatest Guitar Solos of All Time." *Guitar World* Sept. 1998.

Brannin, Summer, and Adam Gimbel. "John Leckie: Studio Stud, July 15, 1998." http://millennianet.com/dumyhead/leckie.html

Bresnark, Robin. *Melody Maker* 30 Aug. 1997.

Brown, Mark. "I Don't Belong Here." *Orange County Register* 1996.

Bryan, Risa. "Anyone Can Play Cards." *Island Ear* 16–23 Aug. 1993.

Bryant, Jerry. Interview with Thom Yorke and Colin Greenwood. *JBTV* June 1993.

Burgess, John. "The Horror! The Horror!" *Jockey Slut* Aug.–Sept. 1998.

Cameron, Keith. "Live: Radiohead." *New Musical Express* Dec. 1992.

———. "Notorious Pig." *New Musical Express* 28 June 1997.

Cantin, Paul. "'Round the Bends." *Ottawa Sun* 25 July 1995.

Cavanagh, David. "It's For You, Jerky!" *Select* May 1993.

Clapps, Albert. "I'm *OK*, Your *OK*." *Stereotype* July 1997.

Clark, Rick. Interview with the author. 23 June, 10 July 1998.

Clark, Stuart. "Transistor Act." *Hotpress* [n.d.].

Collins, Andrew. "Super Creep." *Select* May 1993.

Collis, Clark. "Pulp in Residence." *Select* July 1995.

———. "Radiohead Questionaire." *Select* Jan. 1996.

———. "Videohead." *Select* Oct. 1994.

Considine, J. D. "Harmony in My Head." *Spin* May 1996.

Courtney, Kevin. "Radiohead Calling." *Irish Times* 17 May 1997.

Dalton, Stephen. "The Dour and the Glory." *Vox* Sept. 1997.

Dawn, Randee. "Modulation across the Nation." *Alternative Press* Oct. 1995.

Douridas, Chris. Interview with Thom Yorke. *Morning becomes Eclectic.* KCRW, Santa Monica, 9 June 1997.

Doyle, Tom. "Cheap Thrills." *Melody Maker* 24 Apr. 1993.

———. "Diary of an LP." *Melody Maker* 22 Apr. 1995.

———. "New to Q." *Q* Apr. 1995.

———. "Party On." *Q* June 1997.

Doyle, Tom, et al. "The Hundred Greatest Guitarists of All Time." *Mojo* June 1996.

Dufour, Jean-Francois, et al. *Planet Telex.* 5 June 1998.

> http://www.underworld.net/radiohead/

Du Noyer, Paul. "Cash for Questions: Elvis Costello." *Q* Feb. 1998.

EMI. "Radiohead: Album Biography for *OK Computer*." Press release, May 1997.

Freeman, Paul. "British Quintet Happy to Creep Its Way to Fame." *Barrie Examiner* 8 July 1995.

Freese, Joe. "Pre-Millenium Homesick Aliens." *Wall of Sound.*

> http://www.wallofsound.com/interviews/index.html

Gaitskill, Mary. "Alarms and Surprises." *Alternative Press* Apr. 1998.

Gittens, Ian. Review of Radiohead at Glastonbury. *Melody Maker* 2 July 1994.

Gomez, J. E. "We Haven't Lost Our Independence." *Nightshift* Jan. 1998.

Grant, Kieran. "Radiohead on a Bends-er." *Toronto Sun* 12 Dec. 1995.

Greenwood, Jonny. Interview with the author. 15 Mar. 1996.

Grundy, Gareth. "Stop Whispering, Start Shouting." *Select* Aug. 1998.

———. "The Swamp Songs." *Select* Aug. 1997.

Harding, Nigel. "Interview: Radiohead's Phil Selway." *Consumable* 8 May 1995.

Harkins, Tony. "Welcome to the Instrumental Asylum." *Melody Maker* 27 Nov. 1993.

Harris, John. "Live! On a Friday." *Melody Maker* 22 Feb. 1992.

———. "Radiohead." *Volume 7*. London: World's End, 19 July 1993.

———. "Renaissance Men." *Select* Jan. 1998.

——. Review of *OK Computer*. *Select* July 1997.

——. "Totally Wireless." *Melody Maker* 9 May 1992.

"Have you ever . . ." *Select* Jan. 1998.

Hendrickson, Matt. "Dream Weavers." *Rolling Stone* 16 Oct. 1997.

Hill, Rob. *Bikini* 1997.

Holloway, Alistair. "The Scene Interview: Colin Greenwood." *Scene* 20–26 July 1995.

Howell, Peter. "Paranoia Will Destroy Ya." *Toronto Star* 7 Dec. 1995.

Hughes, Kim. "Radiohead." *Now* 14–20 Aug. 1997.

"The 100 Most Important People in the World." *Select* Dec. 1997.

Interview with Radiohead. *Studio Brussel* 13 June 1997.

Interview Sessions. Chatback Records, 1998.

Irvin, Jim. "Thom Yorke Tells Jim Irvin How *OK Computer* Was Done." *Mojo* July 1997.

Irvin, Jim, and Barney Hoskyns. "We Have Lift-Off." *Mojo* Sept. 1997.

Jennings, David. "Creepshow." *Melody Maker* 25 Sept. 1993.

——. "Jeepers Creepers! Radiohead!" *Melody Maker* 10 Oct. 1992.

Kaufman, Gil. "Drugstore Find Joy on Life's Dark Side." *Sonicnet* 3 June 1998.

Kenny, Glenn. "Single of the Moment: Radiohead." *Rolling Stone* 16 Sept. 1993.

Kent, Nick. Review of *OK Computer*. *Mojo* July 1997.

Kessler, Tim. "'We Never Wanted to Be the Biggest Band in the World.'" *New Musical Express* 13 Dec. 1997.

Kleinedler, Claire. "Don't Call 'Em Britpop." *Addicted to Noise* 1996.

——. Interview with the author. 16 May 1998.

Kulkarni, Neil. "*OK* Compadre." *Melody Maker* 18 Apr. 1998.

Lamacq, Steve. "*Pablo Honey* Album Review." *Select* Apr. 1993.

Lee, Sook Yin. Interview with Radiohead. MuchMusic, June 1997.

Lester, Paul. "From the Bedroom to the Universe." *Melody Maker* 23 Oct. 1993.

Lestor, Paul. "People Have Power." *Uncut* Aug. 1998.

"The Making of *OK Computer*." *Guardian* 20 Dec. 1997.

Malins, Steve. *Coming up for Air*. London: Virgin, 1997.

——. "Scuba Do." *Vox* Apr. 1995.

"The Manna from UNKLE!" *New Musical Express* 22 July 1998.

Masuo, Sandy. "Subterranean Aliens." *Request* Sept. 1997.

McLean, Craig. "Radiohead." *Volume 13*. 1995.

——. "Reviews: Radiohead, *The Bends*." *Vox* Apr. 1995.

Mettler, Mike. "Radiohead: Creeping up the Charts." *Guitar Player* Nov. 1993.

Monk, Katerine. "Touring Cures the Ills Created by Second Album Syndrome." *Vancouver Sun* 6 Apr. 1995.

Moran, Caitlin. "Everything Was Just Fear." *Select* July 1997.

Morgan, Emma. "*OK* Animator." *Select* July 1998.

——. "You Have Been Watching . . ." *Select* June 1998.

Morlin, Caitlin. "Head Cases." *Melody Maker* 10 June 1995.

Morris, Gina. "You've Come a Long Way Baby . . ." *Select* Apr. 1995.

Morrison, Dave. *Select* Apr. 1995.

Mueller, Andrew. "Shiny Unhappy People." *Melody Maker* 28 Oct. 1995.

Mulligan, Terry David. Interview with Thom Yorke and Colin Greenwood. *Much West*. MuchMusic. Aug. 1997.

Muretich, James. "Tuning in with Radiohead." *Calgary Herald* 27 Oct. 1993.

Myers, Caren. "Creep Show." *Mademoiselle* 1995.

——. "Dork Radio." *Details* Nov. 1993.

Nine, Jennifer. "Radio-Unfriendly Unit Shifters." *Melody Maker* 1 Oct. 1994.

——. "Spiders from Mares." *Melody Maker* 18 July 1998.

O'Brien, Ed, Phil Selway, and Colin Greenwood. Interview with the author. 2 June 1997.

Ohler, Shawn. "Radiohead Doesn't Worry if Some Listeners Tune Out." *Edmonton Journal* 20 Mar. 1996.

Oldham, James. "*OK Computer* Album Review." *New Musical Express* 14 June 1997.

Paphides, Peter. "'We're Going to Save Pop Music.'" *Melody Maker* 6 Feb. 1993.

Pareles, Jon. "Miserable and Loving It: It's Just So Very Good to Feel So Very Bad." *New York Times* 2 July 1997.

Pearlman, Nina. "Radiohead: The Morning After." *Rocket* 25 May 1998.

Radiohead: The Interview. Thom Yorke and Colin Greenwood in Conversation. Talking Music, London, 1998.

"Radiohead: The Interview Sessions." Chatback Records. 1998.

"Radiohead Interview: An Exclusive Interview with Colin Greenwood." *Baktabak Interview Collection*. 1998.

"Radiohead: Vive la Megadrive!" *New Musical Express* 3 May 1997.

Pinfield, Matt. Interview with Thom Yorke and Jonny Greenwood. MTV *120 Minutes*. MTV. 19 Apr. 1998.

Randall, Mac. "Radiohead Get the Details." *Musician* Sept. 1997.

——. "The Sounds of '96: 10 Bands You Must Hear." *Musician* Feb. 1996.

Reid, Pat. "Mojo Rising: Radiohead." *Mojo* Apr. 1995.

Richardson, Andy. "Boom! Shake the Gloom!" *New Musical Express* 9 Dec. 1995.

Robbins, Ira. "New Faces: A Guide to This Summer's Coolest Music and the Artists Making It." *Rolling Stone* 8 July 1993.

Ronan. *Curfew* Dec. 1991.

Ross, Mike. "Going 'Round the Bends." *Edmonton Sun* 19 Mar. 1996.

Select Oct. 1994.

Sexton, Paul. "Parlophone Are Confident in Radiohead." *Billboard* 10 May 1997.

sHack. Interview with the author. 15 July 1998.

Sinclair, David. "Thom Yorke: Q and A." *Rolling Stone* 25 Dec. 1997.

Sinclair, Tony. "Head Trip." *Entertainment Weekly* 24 Oct. 1997.

"Single to Damascus Please." *Q* June 1995.

"Stars Shine for Bosnia." *Melody Maker* 2 Sept. 1995.

Steele, Sam. "Sound Bytes: Thom Yorke's Track by Track Guide to *OK Computer*." *Vox* July 1997.

Stoute, Lenny. "Radiohead Is Touring till It Drops." *Toronto Star* 30 Oct. 1993.

——. "Runaway Hit a Mixed Blessing for UK's Radiohead." *Toronto Star* 1 June 1995.

Strauss, Neil. "The Pop Life: Promoting Radiohead." *New York Times* 2 July 1997.

Stud Brothers. "Fame Fatale." *Melody Maker* 11 Mar. 1995.

Sullivan, Caroline. "Bridges and Sighs." *Guardian* 16 May 1997.

Sutcliffe, Phil. "Death Is All Around." *Q* Oct. 1997.

Sutherland, Mark. "Material World: Radiohead." *Vox* Feb. 1996.

——. "Return of the Mac." *Melody Maker* 31 May 1997.

——. "Rounding the Bends." *Melody Maker* 24 May 1997.

Thompson, Dave. "Back to Save the Universe. . . ." *Goldmine* 27 Mar. 1998.

Tourangeau, Clint. "Radiohead Radiate Rock." *See* 14–20 Mar. 1996.

Vaziri, Aidin. "Radiohead: British Pop Aesthetes." *Guitar Player* Oct. 1997.

"Videohead." *Melody Maker* 20 Jan. 1996.

"Vote for Radiohead." *Melody Maker* 17 Feb. 1996.

Wiederhorn, Jon. "Heads across the Sea." *Melody Maker* 31 July 1993.

——. "Live! Radiohead." *Melody Maker* 31 July 1993.

——. "Radiohead Transform Emotional Turmoil into Kinetic Pop." *Rolling Stone* 7 Sept. 1995.

Wilkinson, Roy. "Party of One." *Select* Apr. 1998.

Wylie, Harry. "Radiohead: *OK* Computer." *Total Guitar* Nov. 1997.

Yackoboski, Chris. "Resurfacing with *The Bends*." *What a Magazine* 4 Sept. 1995.

Yorke, Thom. "That's Me in the Corner." *Q* Oct. 1995.

"Yorke Turns Net 'Head." *New Musical Express* 26 Oct. 1996.

Yurkiw, Chris. "Creeped Out." *Mirror* [Montreal] 1 June 1995.